Fingers Pointing to the Moon

FINGERS
pointing to the
MOON

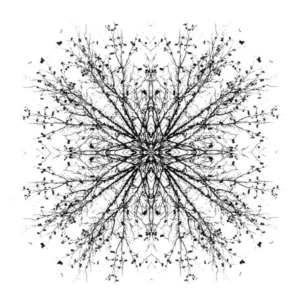

words and images of
Paradox - Common Sense - Whimsy - Transcendence

by Jane English

whose photographs illustrate a best-selling translation of *Tao Te Ching*

Earth Heart • Mount Shasta • California

With gratitude to Earth
and all the friends and teachers she has given me

Published by Earth Heart, Box 7, Mount Shasta, CA 96067   www.eheart.com
Printed in Hong Kong on recycled paper

Photograph on page 61 by Karl Joseph
Upper photograph on page 96 by Sue Steele
Lower photograph on page 96 by Judith English

Quote on page 101 from THE TAO OF PHYSICS by Fritjof Capra, © 1975, 1983, 1991.
Reprinted by arrangement by Shambhala Publications, Inc., Boston.

Quote on page 17 from BEAMTIMES AND LIFETIMES by Sharon Traweek.
Copyright © 1988 by Sharon Traweek
Reprinted by permission of Harvard University Press.

CONTENTS

INTRODUCTION

Sitting down to fill the two remaining blank pages of this book is a task that I have been putting off as long as possible. All the photographs have been chosen and the text has been edited. Now I am to fashion a doorway through which readers can easily enter into what I have created.

Most of the book speaks for itself. The *Table of Contents* gives an overview, and if you leaf quickly through the book you see the rhythm of words and images, and of color and monochrome. I have thoroughly enjoyed the process of making the book over the past few months — poking through old files to find creative pieces from the past thirty years, and letting myself be inspired to write new essays and make new photographs. I find myself smiling every time I pick up the mock-up version of the book that I have made. It is a good book!

There were a few moments when I questioned what I was doing — putting so much personal history and personal favorite images out in a book for all to see. Why does my life warrant a book?

In ways we are all unique, yet all the same. Both the differences and the similarities between my life and yours might be interesting to you. I hope so.

From the fields behind the 1765 colonial house in which I grew up —
the big old elm on the left was planted when the house was built.

As a child I felt at home with nature in the woods and fields behind the house and, though I couldn't put words to it, with the vast realm of spirit towards which the elm seemed to point. The human realm was more problematic. The right-angled human-made form of the house was both a safe haven where I slept, ate and played, and a limitation on nature and spirit. This ambivalence seems to be essential to human existence, the ongoing dance of freedom and constraint in the three worlds spoken of in traditional Chinese writings — heaven, human and nature.

A SCIENCE AUTOBIOGRAPHY

Off to the east the sky shone golden with the first glow of dawn. An old woman wrapped in a blanket sat on a low hill overlooking vast plains. Dry grass covered the gently rolling land, broken only by a thin line of distant railroad tracks and shining telegraph wires that came from the east and stretched off to the western horizon. Once the old woman had gone south to the railroad; the wires had been making a strange singing sound.

The woman was worried about what was happening to her people. The white men had brought with them alcohol and many other diseases of the body and of the soul. Young men were dying in fights with the white men. The death she felt creeping into her old bones was also coming to her people as a whole.

All during the night now ending she had sat in the medicine lodge watching, listening and praying while the old men sat around the fire doing ceremony and urging a return to the old ways. The tribe was weakening, they had said, because the people were not following the old ways of the ancestors. The old woman felt within herself this old knowledge, the ways of the earth, the seasons, the plants and the animals. These ways were good, but now they were not enough. She was tired of hearing the old men say the same things over and over.

She had left the tipi and come to this hill to be alone and talk to spirit directly. Sitting there, she realized that something about the white men's ways fascinated her; there was power in their medicine, a power she felt could help her people.

As her body weakened, her spirit seemed to strengthen. The light in the eastern sky resonated with an inner light she felt more and more. As the sun's first rays came above the horizon, her soul rose out to greet it. She was going home at last. Just as awareness of her body began to drop away, she said joyfully to herself, "I want to learn the ways of the people of the singing wires."

****

In April 1942 I was born in Boston, Massachusetts in a non-labor cesarean delivery. My father was an electrical engineer and my grandfather was a professor at Massachusetts Institute of Technology (MIT). So my beginnings were surrounded by technology, both in the birth and in the family. There also was connection to the natural world. My mother was a gardener, growing both flowers and vegetables, and we lived in an old farmhouse on 40 acres of field and woodland 30 miles north of Boston.

I remember as a child having a flashlight that I took apart over and over to see how it worked. I also watched my father as he made minor electrical repairs such as replacing a defective light switch by the bathroom door in our house. My grandfather had retired from MIT and was a cabinetmaker. He encouraged me to watch him work and gave me wood pieces, a hammer and nails with which I fashioned small boats, trucks and other toys. I also attended an Audubon nature camp and drank in all I could of the natural world. I won the grand prize at the school science fair for my butterfly collection when I was in 7th grade.

Aside from required junior high school science classes and a beginning biology class in my sophomore year of high school, I did not take any science classes until college. I did, however, take four years of math, including beginning calculus. I graduated from high school in 1960.

During my freshman year at Mount Holyoke College I took the introductory physics course for liberal arts students rather than the one for science majors. I had no thoughts of majoring in science. I chose physics rather than chemistry because I thought the chemistry lab smelled bad!

Dorothea Bell, the physics lab instructor, lived in my dorm that year and had the room next to mine. Thus we had many opportunities to become friends. I thoroughly enjoyed the physics lab work; for me it was like having big toys to play with. Dottie noticed my interest and my ability and invited me to do the lab experiments with her on Saturday mornings and then help her teach the lab the following week. Eventually we divided the class with her teaching one experiment two weeks in a row and me teaching another experiment two weeks in a row. The class was divided into two smaller groups that spent time with each of us. During sophomore year I taught the same labs, this time for pay.

When it came time for me to choose a major, Dottie was very helpful, both with advice and as a role model. There were no women physics professors. Over the next two years I progressed easily through the required physics courses. I also assisted in the second year physics lab during my junior year.

During that year, one of the courses I took was an introduction to quantum mechanics. Several of us, including the teacher, found that subject quite confusing on a common sense level, though it hung together logically in its mathematics. We were being told things like, "Light is a wave, light is particles, both and neither all at the same time." When Nobel prize winner Isidor Rabi came to campus to give a lecture, we physics majors were invited to a reception and discussion afterwards. I asked him about this paradoxical state of things in quantum physics, and his answer was that one shouldn't concern oneself about things that cannot be measured or be described mathematically. In other words, I was to ignore my confusion and be satisfied with the mathematical descriptions.

Another visiting lecturer who was an important influence on me was Houston Smith. He was a philosophy professor at MIT and gave a talk on philosophy of science. He had dinner with a group of us at the home of one of our professors and spoke informally of his participation in consciousness research going on at that time at Harvard, including work with psychedelics in the well-known Good Friday experiment on mystical experience, in which graduate students had attended church services, some having ingested LSD (it was still legal at that time) and some taking a placebo. I remember being fascinated but also thinking that I would never do anything like that.

I enjoyed the small group of physics majors. We really became a family, going on hikes together and many of us attending the Unitarian church in Northampton with one of the physics professors. We were introduced to the world of physics research, both on trips to the accelerator laboratory at Princeton where that professor was part of a research group, and on the June "Physics Trips" he and Dottie organized. We visited Bell labs, Goddard Space Flight Center, Oak Ridge, and National Radio Astronomy Observatory, and went to a physics conference at the

University of Wisconsin. Along the way we camped out and visited various points of interest.

Without too much consideration of other paths, I chose to go on to graduate school in physics, accepting a Teaching Assistantship at the University of Wisconsin in the fall of 1964. The course work there was interesting and challenging, though not overly difficult. I ranked 3rd out of 40 on both the Masters level qualifying exam and the PhD preliminary exam. But socially and personally I felt I had run into a stone wall. I had moved from a supportive all-woman environment to one where I was the only woman. All the way through graduate school I was the only woman in any of my classes and research groups.

I received a lot of attention, positive and negative, just for being female. It was hard to tell how I was doing as a physicist, even though my grades were good. Somehow doubt was cast on the appropriateness of my being in physics, and nothing I could do would dispel that shadow. My self-esteem had never been particularly high, and during graduate school it fell considerably. I was the only teaching assistant, among the five or six who worked in the introductory physics course who had to attend all the lectures. The instructor said this was because he needed me to take attendance. I never thought to question this or to suggest that all the teaching assistants take turns doing this chore. Later on, after I had left physics, I was told by another professor who was a friend that the instructor was known to be strongly anti-woman, and that was why he had worked me harder.

During the second year of graduate school I explored a variety of specialties, areas for doctoral research. I spent time with a spectroscopy group and concluded that they were not doing much that was new. Then I spent a summer working with a medical physics group, and again there was not much that was new. It seemed like it was engineering rather than physics that was being done. I intentionally stayed away from high energy particle physics because I had experienced it on trips to Princeton during my undergraduate days. But finally I accepted that that was the field most interesting to me; it really was on the frontier of physics.

My third year in graduate school I was a research assistant in a high energy particle physics group that had professors whose styles seemed friendly to me. One of them, Robert March, was writing an undergraduate text called *Physics for Poets*, all the while doing particle physics research. I participated in a number of bubble chamber experiments at Argonne and Brookhaven National Laboratories. We graduate students designed and built some counters and particle detectors, ran the experiments day-to-day and did data analysis afterwards, lots of supervising film scanners and running computer programs. We also attended seminars and colloquia and occasionally attended national physics conferences. It was strange being the only woman physicist in any of these activities. At parties I felt neither here nor there as I socialized with all-male groups of physicists or all-female groups of wives and girlfriends.

Two events stand out in my memory. Once while I was working at a lathe in the student machine shop, turning lucite light-pipes for a scintillation counter, one of the regular machinists passed the door and glanced in. He skidded to a stop, came back, stared at me, shook his head and went on his way. Another time, at a cocktail hour at a medical physics conference during my second year, one of the professors I was working for came up to me and cautioned me not to get too educated or I wouldn't be able to find a husband.

During my first year, I had met a meteorology graduate student while on a ski trip to Colorado. He was also a good black-and-white photographer and introduced me to darkroom techniques. I took to photography and did a lot of it during my spare time all through graduate school. We both showed and sold lots of prints at student art sales. For me, photographing nature was a way of staying in touch with life in the midst of my technological and theoretical activities in physics.

Another factor in my graduate school years was the political climate. It was during the late 60's and I was surrounded by both Vietnam War protests, complete with tear gas, and the growing hippie counter-culture, with its psychedelics. Being naturally shy, I did not participate in the political activities, though I sometimes had to take a circuitous route to the physics building to avoid tear gas. I felt more akin to the inner explorations of the counter-culture. So there I was, high achieving physics graduate student by day, and photographer and budding hippie evenings and weekends.

One seemingly small event that had a large influence on my life later on was my picking up a copy of Alan Watts' book, *THE BOOK on the Taboo Against Knowing Who You Are.* In this book I found discussions of various Eastern mystical traditions and was struck by the same paradoxical logic I had found in my quantum physics texts while an undergraduate. I avidly read every book by Alan Watts that I could find, and I participated in a "Free University" informal course on mysticism. Then one day as I was reading one of Watts' books something fell apart. I realized that I couldn't find the answer to my confusion in any book. I tossed the book across the room in disgust! I didn't know what to do. In retrospect, I see that my way of proceeding was to increase my photographic work and my inner explorations. I also attended one encounter group weekend. Something in me knew that the answer to my confusion was in nature and in my own being.

Though I could see a big change was coming in my life, I decided to stick it out and finish my PhD. I figured it would open doors for me later on — which it did. My research topic was "Resonance ('particle') Formation in Backward Elastic Anti-Proton/Proton Scattering from 500 to 900 Mev." The data came from bubble chamber film taken at Brookhaven. The results were not earth-shaking, though they did confirm some theoretical predictions of resonance formation at certain specific energies.

During my dissertation research I also helped with the experimental runs for the dissertation research of other graduate students in the group. One of these was an experiment at the Princeton accelerator. I felt as if I were returning home. We graduate students were given a lot of freedom there and used some innovative experimental techniques, feeling somewhat amazed that we lowly graduate students seemed to be in charge a lot of the time.

During graduate school I had live-in relationships with two different physics graduate students, one a nuclear physicist and one in medical physics. I also had a variety of short-term relationships with other physicists. I was an anomaly, being both colleague and part of the group of girlfriends and wives.

Stress was building in my life. It was becoming clear to me that I did not want to live the life of a high energy physicist. It was too competitive and was a great strain for me always being expected to behave in a masculine mode, while being subtly criticized for not being feminine enough. I decided to try to find other things to do as soon as I finished my PhD, with the idea that photography might be a big part of my path.

In retrospect I see that some of the strain was generated simply by attempting to live in the world of high energy physics, a world that Sharon Traweek describes in *Beamtimes and Lifetimes: The World of High Energy Physics* as, "...an extreme culture of objectivity: a culture of no culture, which longs passionately for a world without loose ends, without temperament, gender, nationalism, or other sources of disorder — for a world outside human space and time." (p. 162)

One of the professors in my research group, Ugo Camerini, seemed to me to be a warm human being as well as a good physicist. I spoke with him of some of what I was experiencing and of my decision to explore other paths. His response was very supportive. He suggested that I be assigned as a post-doc to the spark chamber experiment at Lawrence Berkeley Laboratory (LBL) that Wisconsin was doing with University of Hawaii and UC Berkeley. His reasoning was that Berkeley would be a good place for me to explore other possibilities. A lot was going on there at that time.

So in 1970 I went to Berkeley. I remember one day at the Bevatron, the particle accelerator at LBL, I was looking into an oscilloscope as part of tuning up some of the particle detectors. I saw the reflection of my eyes superimposed on the green screen with its bright green traces. I realized that I was more fascinated with the question of just who I was than with the physics I was supposed to be doing. I wondered if I was going crazy. I worked there for 6 months making a lot of new connections in the Bay Area, including one with Stillpoint, a Taoist meditation center in the Santa Cruz mountains run by Gia-fu Feng. He and I immediately felt a special connection between us.

My real point of decision came one morning at dawn after I had been up all night tending the experiment at the Bevatron. I got a phone call from a high energy physics research group at Rutgers offering me a post-doctoral appointment there. As I stood at the outdoor pay-phone and looked at the Golden Gate Bridge lit by the rising sun, I realized that it would be a kind of death for me to take a position in bleak New Brunswick, NJ. I said no to the offer. I trusted that somehow I could make a living with my photography and that I would be able to live, at least for a while, at Stillpoint.

I acted on this decision and by fall of 1970 was living at Stillpoint. After I had been there only a week, feeling joyful and liberated in my new life, I heard from a visitor that some anti-war radicals had set off a bomb in the physics building at Wisconsin where I had just finished graduate work. Such a feeling of bridges burning behind me that evoked! A year or so later, when I was visiting back at Wisconsin, Ugo Camerini told me there were two reasons he was annoyed that I had dropped out of physics. One was that I was being used as an example of why UW should not admit women physics graduate students, and the other reason was that he, Ugo, envied me!

On Christmas day 1970 friends of Gia-fu's arranged for Alan Watts, who had been an Anglican priest, to do a Buddhist wedding ceremony for us. That was the only time I met Alan before his death a few years later.

For the next couple of years I was not active in science. Then around 1973 Gia-fu and I co-taught courses on Chinese Philosophy and Modern Physics at Colorado College, and at Thomas Jefferson College in Michigan. While teaching I felt somehow unqualified to be teaching. I wondered if I hadn't read enough on the subject, but also suspected that no amount of reading and study would be enough. I again felt how a purely intellectual approach was inadequate; there was a gap between words and experience.

While I was with Gia-fu I continued photographing even more intensively. I was delighting in creativity, my own and nature's; I was also reaching for some truth that seemed to be out in nature. This led to our doing translations of the Chinese classics *Tao Te Ching* and *Chuang Tsu: Inner Chapters*, illustrated with Gia-fu's calligraphy and my black-and-white photos. Both books were published by Random House, one in 1972 and the other in 1974. Soon after this, we made a trip to Europe to lead some Tai Chi workshops. There I met the British publisher of *Tao Te Ching* who, noting that I was a physicist, asked me to look over a manuscript that had been submitted to him for publication. It was Fritjof Capra's *Tao of Physics*, which had already been rejected by 11 publishers. I took one look at it, saw that it covered the same ground I had been exploring in the courses I had been teaching, and exclaimed to the publisher, "Of course you are going to publish this!" He invited both Fritjof and me to dinner that night. We met somewhat uneasily, both feeling defensive of our "turf," bringing the competitiveness of high energy physics to this new field where, with eastern philosophy's emphasis on the interconnectedness of things, such competitiveness is quite out of place.

Shortly after this trip, Gia-fu and I went our separate ways. I stayed on at Esalen Institute in Big Sur, CA where we had been visiting friends of his and leading workshops; he returned to Stillpoint in Colorado. While at Esalen I began intensive inner explorations using Gestalt, Rolfing, Tai Chi, chanting, dreamwork, guided imagery and a variety of other body/mind/spirit practices. I had gone from *experimental* physics to *experiential* study of consciousness. One theme that began to emerge for me was the relevance of my non-labor cesarean birth. It seemed to be a factor in my psychological makeup and in my way of relating to people and to the world in general. I kept a journal of my thoughts and experiences.

In the midst of this inner soup, I received an invitation to speak at a conference at UC Santa Cruz on "Energy." It was a real stretch to reassemble something approximating my physicist persona and give the talk, though I did enjoy the process of looking at the roots of the concept of energy and realized that it was just that, a concept, albeit a useful concept.

After almost a year at Esalen I left to participate in a nine month Sensory Awareness study group led by Charlotte Selver, a teacher of Fritz Perls, the founder of Gestalt. In her work we really went back to basics. It was a form of meditation based in awareness of body and had some similarities to Zen meditation. In fact our sessions took place at Green Gulch Farm, a part of San Francisco Zen Center. After a few months of this practice most of us were in very sensitive, open states of being.

In the midst of this I received from the British publisher an almost final version of *Tao of Physics*. I sat down one Sunday afternoon to read it. As I read the phrase, "awareness of atomic reality" something shifted in my being. I actually experienced that awareness. The paradoxical nature of the wave-particle paradox that had been bothering me for 15 years fell away in a transcendent experience where light was not an object that was either wave or particle, and there was no subject (me) seeing light. Neither subject nor object was real. There was just consciousness and the understanding that the ways this seamless unity is divided are conventions, temporary divisions. This experience is more fully described in the chapter, "Science and Transformation," on page 99.

I had earlier had brief moments of this state of consciousness while photographing. I sometimes seemed to become what I was photographing. Such moments were both exhilarating and scary. I had times of wondering if I was going crazy. A few weeks later, during one of the sensory awareness sessions, I came to the understanding that all my photographs are, in a way, self-portraits. They are reflections of my states of consciousness.

Shortly after this I attended a lecture on physics and consciousness and made connection with a group of physicists who met regularly at Lawrence Berkeley Laboratory to discuss research on the relation of physics and consciousness. Fritjof Capra was part of that group. We both commented on the positive changes in each other. Being back at LBL after the major inner changes I was experiencing felt both strange and good.

Meanwhile, my explorations of the personal, social and metaphysical implications of being born non-labor cesarean continued. The process shifted from being just my own personal journey. Several times I noticed people behaving in ways that seemed both unusual and familiar. I subsequently found out that these people were also non-labor cesarean born. Then there were times when I talked with other non-labor cesarean born people about my own experiences and the ways I was conceptualizing them, and these people began to finish sentences for me and make heartfelt exclamations like, "I'm like that too! You mean I'm not crazy?"

One of the things that again emerged, as it had in my physics work and in my photography, was the question of defining inner and outer, subject and object, the question of identity. It seemed that non-labor cesarean born people have a different sense of psychological boundaries, probably from not experiencing the intensely limiting journey down the birth canal. (See the chapter on cesarean birth, page 65, for more.)

All this while I was aware of an inner voice telling me that this cesarean work I was doing wasn't very scientific. It was too subjective and not scientifically verified. But the inner motivation to heal myself and the excitement of feeling I was onto something new kept me going. Meeting Stanislav Grof, a Czech psychiatrist whose research in psychedelics had led him to a detailed topography of the perinatal experience for vaginal birth, inspired me to begin to map the cesarean experience in a similar way.

Stan also was my introduction to transpersonal psychology, areas of study that go beyond the individual psyche and explore the border between the personal and the spiritual. I also became acquainted with Charles Tart's idea of "state-specific science" wherein the state of consciousness of the scientist-observer is an important factor in what is observed. My own work began to look a bit more scientific, and therefore valid. I still subscribed to a scientific worldview with science being the criterion for validity. Houston Smith reappeared in my circle of acquaintances, and I found his writings on science, spirit and perennial philosophy quite helpful.

In the late 1970's and early 1980's I was recording my dreams, doing daily meditation and using the Tarot as an oracular mirror of inner states of consciousness. I began to notice amazing correlations between the dream images I was writing down and the images on the Tarot cards I would choose *after* doing the writing. This challenged the scientific voice that said that the choice of cards was random. Being still a scientist at heart, I proceeded to do a statistical analysis to find the probability that the frequency distribution of the cards I had chosen over a three year period was random. It was far from random, as were those of two other Tarot practioners' cards. I did control runs with numbered index cards, using the same shuffle procedure. The only other difference was that I was not meditating just before the choice. I also did controls with a computer random number generator. Both controls were consistent with randomness. See the chapter "Tarot and Physics" on page 49 for more on this. This was a major step in integrating my inner work with my scientific training.

In the 1980's, my continued exploration of cesarean birth, including giving talks at several psychology conferences, led me to learning shamanic techniques with Michael Harner. I learned that traditional shamans had explored the inner realms of consciousness and their interface with the manifest physical world with the same intensity and precision that high energy physicists use in the world of sub-atomic particles. It was interesting to hear a visiting Hungarian anthropologist say that in his language the word for "scientist" and that for "shaman" are the same word!

Over the past few years, my association with spiritual cosmologist and visionary artist Rowena Pattee Kryder has helped me to see science in a larger perspective. Rather than seeing science as the ultimate arbiter of reality, a container for everything true, I now find it more accurate to know science as a part of a much larger reality, a reality with spiritual, human, natural and cultural dimensions, a reality that cannot always be put into words or mathematics or even images.

This understanding was foreshadowed by a dream I had in 1978 while I was auditing a course with Angeles Arrien on creativity and perception. In the dream I was sitting in a beautiful garden with a young girl. Several men who were physicists were having a serious discussion. They wore grey suits and were going into a grey stone building that had columns across the front, a temple-like hall of science perhaps. The girl was upset that we were not allowed in there. I explained to her that this was because we were female. Then we danced among the flowers and realized that we were happy not having to go into that grey building.

Liberated from the authority of orthodox science, I find myself working toward integrating "the old ways" and "the ways of the people of the singing wires." This book is a part of that process.

I like using patterns from nature as the basis for mandalas. There is a richness that is not present in forms that are totally human-made.

The 45 degree slice at the right is from a photo of a sycamore tree. To form the mandala above I placed it eight times, rotating and mirroring it each time. The mandala to the right was formed from the same slice, but the slice was colored in before it was placed eight times.

PHOTOGRAPHY: THE INWARD JOURNEY

In 1982 I was invited to give a five minute slide show as part of a longer program. I decided to make a history of the ways I have experienced photography. 64 slides were shown quickly, almost as a movie while I read the text. Selected images, including some more recent ones, accompany the complete text here. Note that parts of the text go with photos not shown here.

I am going to share with you my personal journey in photography. I hope to do so in a way that touches something universal and resonates with the journey each of you is on, with the path you are following. I include both color and black-and-white photographs, also some paintings.

Coming into physical form, incarnating, is an experience of falling away from union with a perfection that is beyond light, but which is often spoken of as light. In retrospect, I see that I was unconsciously reaching back for that light in much of my photography work. I was mistaking the outer world light for the inner light. Often there has been a feeling of sadness or longing in my photographing. I believed that the light was out there separate from me rather than within.

As a child I spent much time out in the woods lying on the ground looking up through the trees. I felt connected with something I had no name for. I also remember lying under our Christmas tree looking up at the branches and the colored lights, feeling a sense of ecstasy and perfection.

Photography was a part of life in my family. My grandfather did his own developing and printing in the early part of this century, and my father took pictures of mountains and scenery on our vacations.

Photographing was a way of reaching out and touching the natural world from which our 20th century technological civilization was rapidly separating us. This reaching out to nature is evident in even this snapshot I made when I was eighteen.

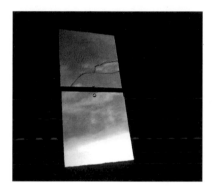

While in graduate school in the late 1960's, I began intensive photographic work simultaneously with intensive work in physics. The conventional scientific worldview deepened in me the splits between intuition and reason and between inner and outer.

Photographing was for me an unconscious attempt to heal myself. Photographing allowed me to play in nature as I had as a child. Holding a camera took care of the need to be doing something and allowed the rest of me to just be.

I often imagined my photographs as being like Chinese paintings, so when Gia-fu Feng and I were working on a translation of *Tao Te Ching* it felt natural to us for him to do his calligraphy right on the photographs, in the style of Chinese paintings.

I had little previous knowledge of oriental philosophy and religion, so the great success of the book catapulted me into a whole new world.

My scientific belief system slowly gave way,

and disintegrated!

For quite a few years I
felt lost and confused.

Yet I was aware that a new direction and a
new sense of being alive was slowly emerging.

During this time my attention was focused inward and I did very little photographing. That which I did do was from a deeper place in myself.

During that difficult period of self-exploration I finally became aware of how much I projected my sense of beauty onto nature, which I then photographed in an attempt to re-own it.

I realized that all my photographs are in some sense self-portraits, are external mirrors of internal states, most of which don't even have names.

Inner images and experiences gradually became more important to me than images of the external world. In an attempt to communicate these inner images that came from a place where I couldn't take my camera, I learned to paint.

A real turning point came for me when in 1978 I left my darkroom and 15 years of photographic work in Mendocino, California and moved down the coast to San Francisco to take some classes from Angeles Arrien and Ralph Metzner. About a week after I moved to San Francisco, my darkroom back in Mendocino burned. With it went all my negatives and all my equipment, except for the camera I had brought with me. *(Note: this photo is not of my darkroom burning but it gives the feeling!)*

Though I don't recommend experiencing a fire, it certainly was a transformative time for me. It was an outer mirror of an inner change, a change I had resisted until the external event forced me to look at it.

My old kind of seeing involved being disconnected from awareness of body and emotion, and projecting all my awareness out onto nature. The photographs I made were beautiful enough, but in making them I was often splitting myself.

The old seeing died with the fire. The emotional pain became water that nourished the tree of life, increased awareness of body, and brought me back to myself. The tree now begins to support a more integrated seeing, one in which I see with my heart and body as well as with my head and eyes.

And I began to photograph people, something I'd never been comfortable with before. I began to experience people with the same clarity with which I've always seen nature. I began to see the same light in people that I've always seen in nature. Both humans and nature are manifestations of a universal light that is also within me.

As a photographer I am an artist whose paint is light and whose brushes are trees, flowers, clouds and human faces.

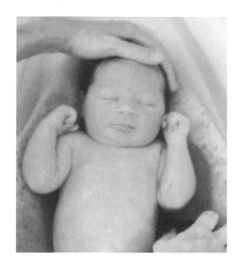

Light, instead of being something outside me, begins also to be inner light. Sometimes I even go beyond the idea that works of art are objects and realize that living life as a human is actually the highest art form of all.

This doesn't mean losing the magic of images, rather it is allowing the magical and spiritual to become one with the mundane and ordinary.

As long as there are images, of the outer world or of inner visions, there is still an experience of separateness.

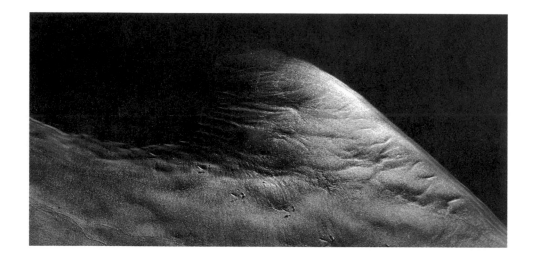

But at times all the images go and there is only presence.

And, as in life another inhalation follows each exhalation, the images return.

Barra de Navidad, Mexico -- January 1976

After sunset
        Almost too dark to see
                Beach waves pounding

        Evening stillness

The last bathers retreat to their lighted houses
        I sit alone

        Sky red along the edge

A large dark bird silently flies over
        the still, faintly orange-blue moving water
Lands in the wash of a wave and walks slowly up to
        where only the fingertips
                of an occasional wave touch its feet

One   slow   step

Another

De   lib   er   ate   ly

It walks. sometimes disappearing against a dark wave
        then silhouetted black against silver beach water

I wait   Expecting

What is it that I am expecting?   I don't know

I stand, walk to my lighted house, and write this

My first camera was given to me by my grandfather. It was a little Kodak Brownie box camera with no exposure controls other than the shutter. It used black-and-white film. This was a good beginning for me, as much of my later color photography has a solid foundation in the black-and-white work; most of my color photos would also look good in black-and-white.

I like to use color sparingly, as an accent, a point of intensity. Perhaps my single-minded pursuit of Girl Scout merit badges as a child was as much to get yet another colorful embroidered badge as it was to learn the required skills!

48

TAROT AND PHYSICS

This paper was originally written in a scientific format. Here, even though this is not a scientific journal, I have decided to stay with that form, perhaps to honor one of the cultural rituals of the scientific community!

Abstract

After using Tarot cards daily for several years as part of a meditation and self-reflection practice, Jane English, a Ph.D. physicist felt both personal and scientific need to reconcile her Tarot experience with her scientific worldview. Statistical analysis of cards chosen daily in meditation for three years from 1978 to 1981 (one card for "body," one for "mind" and one for "spirit") shows 99.97% probability of their being non-random. Analysis of cards similarly chosen by two other Tarot practitioners shows even greater non-randomness. Control experiments done with numbered index cards and with a computer random number generator are consistent with randomness. The deciding factor in producing the non-random results is that cards depicting powerful archetypes be chosen from an expanded state of consciousness after a period of meditation.

Australian physicist Brian McCusker has replicated the experiment a number of times with several people and shows similar results. At Jane English's suggestion he also analyzed his data separately for the body, mind and spirit cards. As she hypothesized, the results were increasingly non-random as one goes from the subject/object world of the physical body, through the intermediate world of mind, to the unitive world of spirit.

This simple experiment can be replicated by anyone willing to make the effort.

Introduction

It is commonly thought that science is incompatible with Tarot, that science is totally logical while Tarot is totally intuitive. For a long time, I too was of this opinion and, being committed to a scientific worldview, would have nothing to do with Tarot. I saw it as mere fortune-telling, as something used by the unscrupulous to manipulate and control those who were too lazy to take responsibility for their lives. However, some years after I became as interested in exploring the inner worlds of consciousness as I had been in exploring the outer world scientifically, I met and studied with people who were using Tarot in a way that appealed to me. They used it as a mirror of consciousness and as a tool for growth and transformation.

Using Tarot

I found that Tarot helped me to focus intuition and perception and to find within myself a deep and true kind of knowing. It helped me to perceive aspects of myself and of the world of which I am not ordinarily aware. I used it as a tool, a mirror for clarifying and getting new perspective on situations in my life.

As I began to use the cards I often had a vague sense of uncanny accuracy in the three cards I chose daily as a part of a meditation. Each day I picked cards to represent body, mind and spirit aspects of myself. When I turned over the cards I had chosen face down and saw which ones they were, they usually seemed absolutely appropriate to my present situation. Often they brought into full awareness something of which I was only half aware. Sometimes the connection between the cards and my situation was very specific and sometimes more general. The following examples of dreams and Tarot cards illustrate this connection. I used the Crowley-Thoth deck. I wrote the dreams in my journal *before* choosing the day's cards.

Dream: Water with green slime in it is poured over me.
Tarot Card: Seven of Cups—Cups overflowing with green slimy water.

Dream: With paper and charcoal, I am making a rubbing of a stone that has a bumblebee and an elegant lady carved in it.
Tarot Card: The Empress—An elegant lady with bumblebees embroidered on her shirt.

Dream: The water coming from a garden hose I am using slows to a dribble. I follow the hose back and discover that it is not connected to any source.
Tarot Card: Eight of Cups—Only four of the eight cups are being filled with water. The flower stems are not rooted in the earth. This is a similar image of reduced flow and disconnection from a source.

Dream: A house I have lived in and a car I have driven are both burning. I am not afraid.
Tarot Card: Princess of Wands—Swirls of fire and the fearless lady with the tiger by the tail. Flowers that symbolize aspects of one's identity that are no longer needed are burning on a pedestal.
Connection: Cars and houses are also symbols of identity. In both the dream and the card, symbols of identity are burning, and this is happening without fear.

Dream: I am with a friend who is one of my teachers. We have a bowl full of cookie dough and half-formed cookies. We meditate before starting to work on the cookies. As I start to reach for the dough, he asks that we meditate more. I close my eyes and experience light, stars, colors, and patterns of energy. I feel our unity as energy. I no longer have an identity; there is no sense of "me," just consciousness and energy. There is awareness that he and I are in this experience together. We are the experience, the awareness.

Tarot Cards: The Tower—In the "body" position of the spread. A fire-breathing dragon destroying the tower, a symbol of identity. Human figures falling from the tower, symbols of personality images being cleared away. An eye above, a symbol of clear vision of one's true self.

Three of Wands—In the "mind" position. Orange and white flames and open lotus flowers, symbols of integrity and wholeness in one's perception of self and others.

Ace of Wands—In the "spirit" position. The torch of fire, a symbol of the ability to burn out obstacles in consciousness and to go beyond conditioning.

Connections: Light, fire, vision, energy, and transcendence in both dream and cards.

"Scientific" Doubts

Reconciling my experience of the cards as mirrors with my scientific training that views external things as really separate from ourselves was a slow and difficult process for me. From an orthodox scientific perspective the Dream/Tarot correlations would be seen as too subjective to be good data. Most scientists would say that the cards are separate from the person who chose them, that they were chosen in a random way, and that therefore the cards could not have a meaningful connection to the person's subjective reality. Connections like those in the Dream/Tarot examples would be seen as the result of imagination and chance, and therefore not to be considered real. Scientists say the cards and the person are separate so the choices are random, and Tarot practitioners say the cards and the person are connected so the choices are not random.

Being both a scientist and a Tarot practitioner, I was intensely interested in resolving this conflict! Having experienced much that is useful and valuable in using the tools of both science and Tarot, I was interested in integrating these two areas of my experience. I decided to apply one of the tools of science to my Tarot experience. I did a statistical analysis of my records of the Tarot cards I had chosen in meditation for a period of two years. Two friends, whom I will call B and C, had followed a similar practice and had records of cards chosen over two and three years, respectively. They lent me their records so I could do a statistical analysis of the cards they had chosen.

Statistical analysis is a tool used in science to test the relative validity of conflicting hypotheses, conflicting theoretical explanations of phenomena observed in experiments. As such, it was ideally suited to seeing which was more valid, science's claim that choosing Tarot cards is random or Tarot's claim that it is not random.

I had much mental and emotional resistance to doing the statistics. I knew that I would feel stuck with the results. Either it would affirm my old scientific worldview that I was beginning to find too narrow, or it would force it to change and set me off into the unknown.

The Importance of Subjective Data

When exploring something, like the use of Tarot, that is related to both subjective and objective experience, it is important to include subjective data along with the objective data. The following material is the subjective data associated with the records of the Tarot cards chosen.

As I did my three-card spread each day, I expected that the cards chosen would mirror my state of consciousness. I chose them after a period of shuffling that served primarily as a concentration device as I focused my awareness on myself and the coming day. The shuffle was only secondarily a way of randomizing the cards. This focusing of awareness was not a narrowing of attention, the usual thinking about or concentrating on something. On the contrary, it was an expansion, a relaxing that allowed new thoughts, emotions, intuitions, sensations, and sometimes a sense of quiet emptiness to emerge into awareness.

After the shuffle, I then spread out the cards face down in a fan. Following an inner sense of appropriateness, I chose three cards to represent body, mind, and spirit. Sometimes my eyes and hand seemed drawn to a particular card. I knew it was right when my whole being seemed to say "yes." The "yes" is the verbal component of an experience that involves thoughts, emotions, intuitive images, and physical sensations. At the time of doing most of the spreads, I had no intention either of trying to guess what cards I was choosing or of eventually subjecting the cards chosen to a statistical analysis.

Person B says that during the shuffle, she becomes very quiet and clear. She feels that everything is on hold. She sometimes shuffles for as long as five minutes before spreading out the cards face down in a fan. She has a variety of ways of choosing the cards. Sometimes she runs the palm of her hand above the cards without touching them and at certain cards experiences a sensation that to her means "stop." At other times she uses one of her fingers rather than her palm to choose in a similar manner. At times her eyes seem drawn to a particular card. Occasionally, instead of feeling a sensation, she notices that her breathing becomes irregular or that she feels very clear as her hand, fingers, or eyes approach a certain card. She may not immediately pick a card that comes to her attention in one of these ways. She may move on to other cards and then come back to the original card to see if what she calls the "charge" is still there. She may experience charge with several cards before deciding which three to choose.

Person C says that she chooses her cards each morning. She usually spends ten to fifteen minutes on a spread. She shuffles the entire deck, then divides it into three stacks. She then shuffles each stack individually and makes a fan of it. There is always one card in each stack that her eyes are instantly attracted to. About half the time, the cards mirror to her either what is going on in the physical world at that time, what she is thinking about, or what she is feeling. And half the time, she doesn't immediately see any significance in the spread. But she says that as the day progresses, she can see a correlation between the spread and what she is experiencing.

Statistical Analysis of the Cards Chosen

The question being considered is, "Are the choices of Tarot cards done as described above random, or are they not random?" The following procedure is a way of deciding that question by calculating the probability that they are not random.

Definition of e — the expected frequency: If the choices are random, the probability in any one choice of picking any one of the 78 cards in the deck is exactly equal to the probability of picking any other of the 78 cards and is equal to $1/78$. When a large number "N" of choices is made, the expected number of times "e" that a particular card is chosen is defined as $e = N/78$; "e" is called the expected frequency.

Definition of f_i — the actual frequency: Anyone who has rolled dice knows that on the average, each number comes up $1/6$ of the time, but that for a finite number "M" of rolls the actual number of times each number appears varies widely from $M/6$, even when the dice aren't loaded! Similarly, the actual number of times card "i" is chosen from the 78 Tarot cards will vary widely from $N/78$, even if the choices are random. The actual number of times card "i" is chosen is called the actual frequency and is labeled "f_i." The group of 78 numbers f_i for i = I to 78 is called the frequency distribution of the cards chosen.

Definition of X^2: In statistical work the quantity X^2 (chi-square) is used as an overall measure of the variation, in a frequency distribution, of the actual frequencies f_i from the expected frequency e. The following equation is the definition of X^2

$$X^2 = \sum_{i=1}^{78} \frac{(f_i-e)^2}{e} = \frac{(f_1-e)^2}{e} + \frac{(f_2-e)^2}{e} + \frac{(f_3-e)^2}{e} + \ldots + \frac{(f_{78}-e)^2}{e}$$

Finding P — the probability of non-randomness: Statistics texts contain tables showing the probability "P" that a frequency distribution with a certain value of X^2 is not the result of random choice. From the records kept by myself (person A) and by persons B and C, I counted N (the total number of cards chosen by that person) and all 78 of the f_i (the actual number of times each of the 78 cards was chosen by that person). Using these numbers, I calculated "e" and then X^2 for each person. Then by using the tables, I found a value of P for each person. Figure 1 shows these values of N, X^2, and P.

Controls: As a control, I made a pack of 78 index cards, blank on one side and numbered 1 to 78 on the other. Using the same kind of shuffle procedure I had used with the Tarot cards, I chose the same number N cards, three cards at a time, recorded them, and did the same statistical test for non-randomness. The only difference was that I chose them all in a period of a few hours and not as part of a meditation. The results of this are shown in Figure 2. As a further check I programmed an Apple II computer to perform the same process. The results of this are shown in Figure 3.

Results: In most statistical work, probabilities of either 95% or 99% are considered sufficient for an effect to be considered real. So the data in Figures 1, 2, and 3 certainly constitute evidence that something other than random chance was operating in the choice of Tarot cards in meditation, and that the index-card and computer choices can be considered random.

Tarot cards by person	N	X^2	P
A	1982	127.3	99.97%
B	2015	1161.0	99.999...% (100×10^{-10})
C	2395	132.4	99.99%

Figure 1

Index Cards	N	X^2	P
	1982	85.83	53%

Figure 2

Apple computer	N	X^2	P
I	1410	82.5	50%
2	1680	88.5	65%
3	1821	59.2	*
4	1983	70.84	*
5	1983	66.04	*
6	1983	102.31	94.8% (see note p.60)
7	1983	58.64	*
8	1983	71.63	*
9	1410	66.9	*
10	1680	69.7	*
11	1821	79.8	*
12	2052	85.9	53%
13	2394	85.8	53%

* = less than 50%

Figure 3

Interpretation of the Statistical Analysis

This statistical analysis exemplifies one of the positive aspects of science. You follow your doubts in a systematic way as far as you can. Then when you have finished with this, you are stuck with the reality of your results. There is no room for further doubt. I used statistical analysis, one of the tools of science, to measure the probability of non-randomness in the choice of Tarot cards.

Saying the choice is random is the same as saying that the cards are totally separate from the person who picks them. Saying the choice is not random is to say there is a connection between the person and the cards. After doing all the analysis, I was stuck with the reality of the connectedness of the Tarot cards and the person who chooses them in meditation, even though my old scientific belief system asserted that there was no connection. The statistical analysis doesn't show the nature of the connection between the person and the cards; it just shows that it is very probable that there is a connection of some kind.

This evidence of a connection can be interpreted in a variety of ways. One possibility is that we cheated in some way, that we peeked at the cards or that their backs were marked. But the fact that, except for 29% of my own data (person A), the Tarot cards were chosen without any intention of subjecting them to a statistical analysis provides a reason why we would have no motivation to cheat. It is also possible that the shuffle was not sufficient to make the choices random. However, the index-card data make this possibility seem quite unlikely.

Another possibility is that some kind of psychic or ESP process was happening. Remembering that in the process of choosing the cards, physical sensation was involved in the experience of "yes," one could say that the cards are perceived by some kind of sixth sense. My objection to this kind of explanation is that calling it psychic mystifies the experience of direct intuitive knowing, an experience that really is quite common and ordinary. Introducing an "ESP mechanism" is an unnecessary complication.

I prefer to interpret the statistical analysis and the Dream/Tarot correlations as showing that there is some kind of subtle connectedness, resonance or direct knowing involved. This is far more simple and elegant than hypothesizing more mechanisms of perception. Direct knowing is a dissolving of boundaries and a merging of identities. We experience the cards as if they were part of ourselves. The assumption that the cards are separate from us is what underlies the "scientific" belief that the choices are random. On a gross physical level the cards can be seen as separate, other than the physical connection from the cards on the table through the table legs, down into the floor and up into our bodies through the chairs. But that is not the kind of connection referred to in direct knowing. The connection is more subtle, at a deeper level of reality that underlies the physical level.

The interpretation of the data as implying a deeper kind of connectedness supports the evolving worldview of Tarot practitioners, the belief that the external world and inner states of consciousness mirror and reflect each other. The Tarot cards form a microcosm in which this reflection is clearer than in everyday life. Having been created by many people over a long period of time, Tarot is a good mirror with few distortions. It is easier to see the reflection symbolically in the cards than in the complex events of life.

The next step in this evolving worldview is to go beyond the inner/outer split and find that the totality of one's experience is coherent, is based on unity of some kind. It seems that separation is an appearance, an illusion that we can play with and enjoy, rather than being something absolute.

A Replication of This Experiment

A copy of an unpublished report on this material was noticed in 1986 by Australian physicist Brian McCusker. He had two people replicate the experiment for one year with the following results (McCusker, 1988) (figure 4):

Tarot cards by person	N	X^2	P
D	1095	141.3	1.4×10^{-5}
E	1095	282	10^{-24}

figure 4

Both D and E did control sets of shuffling and card choosing with regular playing cards and obtained results consistent with randomness for these. Person E continued the experiment for two more years (figure 5).

	N	X^2	P
E - 3 yr. run	3288	1177	3×10^{-109}

figure 5

Hypothesizing that the degree of non-randomness (that is, the degree of connectedness) would increase as one focuses first on the physical world of discrete objects for the body card, then for the mind card on the world of thought which is non-physical but still subject-object oriented and finally for the spirit card on a unitive world of oneness beyond any subject-object split, the present author (Jane English) suggested to Brian McCusker that he do separate analysis for the body cards, for the mind cards, and for the spirit cards from person E's three year run. He did so with results that confirm the hypothesis (McCusker, 1990) (figure 6):

	N	X^2	P
Body cards	1096	419.9	5×10^{-34}
Mind cards	1096	438.8	4×10^{-36}
Spirit cards	1096	531.9	6×10^{-46}

figure 6

It is especially interesting that the idea of doing separate analysis for the body, mind and spirit cards did not even occur until after the experiment was complete, making it unlikely that there was any bias on the part of person E.

A Note on Oracles

Tarot is an example of an oracle, as are I Ching, The Runes, The Medicine Cards, The Gaia Matrix Oracle and numerous other systems. An oracle is a symbol system that is an integrated map of the archetypes present in our individual and collective psyches. Daily use of an oracle is like a look in the mirror each morning, only it is a look at the deeper levels of the psyche. This experiment could be repeated using any of these oracles. Probably the non-randomness would be highest when a person uses an oracle that has personal meaning for them.

Conclusion

This experiment is one that anyone can do; no expensive laboratory equipment is needed. But it is not necessarily an easy experiment. Daily discipline is needed, as is the willingness to be changed by the doing of the experiment. The combination of daily meditation and conscious interaction with a powerful collection of archetypes cannot help being a deep adventure in self-exploration and transformation. To do this experiment one must grow beyond identifying oneself as an "objective" scientist and become a "new scientist" who is committed to truth in a very broad sense.

References

McCusker, Brian and Cherie Sutherland McCusker. (1988). "An Experimental Test of the Basis of Probability Theory", *The Australian Physicist*, vol.25 #1, Jan/Feb 1988, pp. 20-24.

McCusker, Brian. (1990). private communication.

Note

Run #6 in the Apple computer data on p. 56 has a non-randomness probability of 94.8%. This is barely below 95%, the conventional level of significance. All the other runs have 65% or less probability of being non-random. Note also that run #7 has the lowest X^2 and so the lowest probability of non-randomness of all. As an interesting anecdote I will describe here what my subjective state was while the computer was doing those two runs. This was in the early days of personal computers and each run took over a minute.

On seeing run after run come out consistent with randomness during the first five runs I realized that there really was something different going on when Tarot card choices were made after meditation, rather than quickly with the index cards or the computer runs. I felt myself fully accept that there was a significant effect, a kind of connectedness happening during the use of the Tarot cards after meditation.

I sat there experiencing this sense of connectedness while the computer was doing run #6. Much to my surprise that run came out very close to being significantly non-random, in other words, "connected" to my state of consciousness. I had had no intention of influencing the computer.

Being still a scientist, I said to myself, "OK, so if that is "connectedness," I'll now go into a state of "separateness" for run #7 and see what happens. Going from connectedness to separateness can be best described as sort of like taking off a jacket, deliberately removing something. Run #7 done while I was in this state of "separateness" came out the least probably non-random, or the most probably random, of any of the runs.

Interesting experience! This is not scientific data but seemed worth mentioning here.

Science meets Intuition

The First Cesarean Birth

based on my shamanic journey experience in 1984

In a cave part way up the side of a valley a small group of people sit around an open fire. It is early spring at the end of a long hard winter. Several members of this small band of people have died during the winter. The others are weak but glad to see the beginnings of spring.

Until this night they had also been happy about the imminent birth of a child to one of the women. But the mood is somber as they sit around the fire, for the woman lying on some furs is near death after a long hard labor. The child has not been born. It seems that not only is there not to be a birth but there will be one more death. The band is getting so small it may not survive.

Across the fire from where the young woman lies is an older woman whose hair is beginning to grey. She is the keeper of the knowledge of herbs for this band and is consulted in all health matters. She suddenly sits up straighter and peers intently at the younger woman lying there. She can see no movement of breathing; perhaps death has already come. Reaching into her leather pouch for an obsidian stone she uses for cutting leather, she stands and silently walks toward the young woman.

Telepathically she communicates to the young woman not to be afraid. She sees that the woman's soul has indeed left the body and is hovering there above the fire. Gently the older woman pulls aside the furs and leather dress covering the young woman's belly. Carefully she cuts open the belly a layer at a time, finds the head of the child, and lifts it out. By now other women have come to assist her as she delivers the child. All are awed, some are afraid, but they trust the older woman. The child cries and breathes jerkily as the women clean him off and wrap him in soft furs. The older woman motions another young woman who is the mother of a one-year-old to take the newborn and nurse him.

The older woman puts herbs, maybe sage, into the wound and thanks the great earth-mother-goddess for this new life and for the vision of how to safely deliver the baby from its dead mother's body. Perhaps the older woman remembered seeing living baby rabbits come from the cut open belly of a pregnant rabbit whom the woman had killed with a rock from her sling.

This small band of people has lost yet another adult, but it has a new child. And it has new knowledge, a new way of giving birth.

Birth Poem - March 9, 1981

Snail squirming grey slime
        Tail long in water
                Forming
                Unforming

Clear starlight silver shimmer
        Soft fire above me

Breath exploding in fragments of light
        Expanding to the limits of the universe
                Disintegrating
                Dying

Heavy stone
        Holding me against the explosion of
                Light & Touch & Sound & Breath
                A cool still dark center

I am

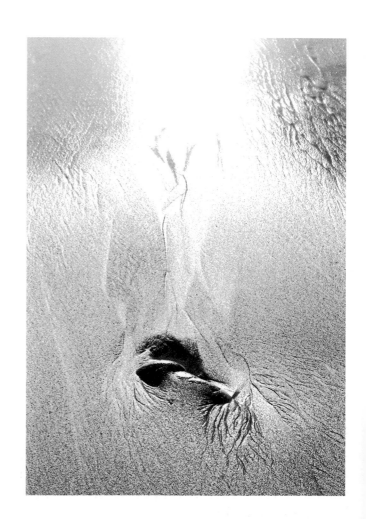

FOUR PERSPECTIVES ON BEING BORN CESAREAN

A talk at the Congress of the International Society for Pre and Perinatal Psychology and Medicine in Heidelberg, Germany, May 1995

The four perspectives of thesis, antithesis, synthesis and metathesis or transcendence are applied here to my work on cesarean birth. They can equally well be applied in many other areas. I begin with the abstract that was published in the conference proceedings. It gives a good overview. Following that is an edited transcript of the actual talk.

Abstract:

As conception and birth become increasingly technological with *in-vitro* conception, surrogate motherhood, cesarean birth and neo-natal intensive care, it becomes important to listen to the people whose entry into human form was technologically assisted. With cesarean birth being one of the earliest forms of modern birth technology, cesarean born people have had time to attain maturity and have begun to speak of their experiences. Listening to them is important not only for understanding cesarean birth, but also as a first step toward understanding the experience and worldview of all who had technological assistance in coming to Earth.

During the 20 years of research, self-exploration and collecting anecdotal material that led to her book, *Different Doorway: Adventures of a Caesarean Born*, and to her paper, "Being Born Cesarean: Physical and Psychosocial Aspects" (*Pre and Perinatal Psychology Journal*, vol.7 #3), Jane English looked at cesarean birth through a variety of conceptual frameworks, each with a different viewpoint and emphasis.

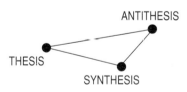

Her scientific training led her initially to frame her inquiry with the question, "What are the effects of having been born cesarean?" This traditional cause-and-effect, mechanistic perspective was helpful in gathering knowledge of what the experience of cesarean birth is like from the child's point of view and how this experience could be an imprint that influenced later personality development. The limitation of this perspective was that it tended to support feelings of irresponsibility and not having control of life.

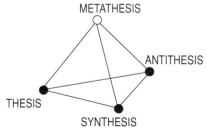

Further inner exploration and reading led her to apparent past-life experiences and to the possibility that not only is cesarean birth a cause of personality traits but is itself an effect of them. Widening her view of being human beyond the limits of physical embodiment led to the consideration that the most congruent method of incarnating specific soul intentions and/or karmic patterns might in some cases be a cesarean birth. The limitation of this perspective is a sense of being not only responsible for but to blame for everything experienced in this life.

Moving beyond cause-and-effect and a sense of linear time, and being inspired by various humanistic and transformational psychologies, led to a third perspective. Simple non-judgmental acceptance of the experience of being born cesarean became a powerful tool for personal growth and transformation. The eventual limitation of this perspective was a sense of being OK only when changing, growing or transforming.

Inspired by her experience of the quantum mechanical wave-particle paradox (see the chapter "Science and Transformation") as a "zen koan," a riddle whose answer is an experience, not words, a fourth "perspective" emerged. This was going beyond the subject-object split and understanding that consciousness and identity transcend the physical body, particular ways of being born and individual lifetimes. The only potential difficulty with this was lapsing into worrying that nothing was real, that all these ideas about cesarean birth were illusions. (Which they are, as are all ideas, from a transcendent perspective!)

All these stances are useful at particular moments. None is inherently better than the other; mastery comes in taking them appropriately. As noted above they all can have distorted shadow sides.

The following outline summarizes these four perspectives. These are all stances that the author experienced during her journey. They are all useful at appropriate moments. No one is better than the others; mastery comes in taking them appropriately. They all have shadow sides that are distortions or contractions.

THESIS
Being born cesarean causes certain personality traits.
"I am the way I am because I was born cesarean."
Shadow side: "I am shaped by events over which I had no control
so I'm not responsible for how I am."

ANTITHESIS
There are certain karmic patterns or soul intentions
that cause a cesarean birth.
"I was born cesarean because of what I experienced in a past life."
"I create my reality."
Shadow side: "I am to blame for everything I experience."

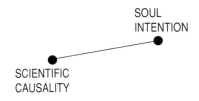

SYNTHESIS
Non-judgmental acceptance of the experience of being born cesarean
is a powerful tool for personal growth and transformation.
"Cesarean birth is part of my 'native' culture;
my past is 'compost' for my future."
"Cesarean born and vaginally born, we have been given birth,
given life, breath, heartbeat and a chance to be on Earth."
Shadow side: "I am OK only when I am transforming myself."

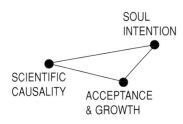

METATHESIS (Transcendence)
From an expanded state of consciousness, identity transcends
the physical body, ways of being born, and individual lifetimes.
"I – Not I – All is delight."
Shadow side: "Nothing is real.
All my ideas about cesarean birth are false."

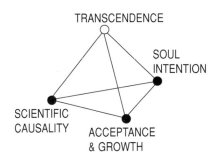

The talk:

My own background is not in psychology, not in a medical profession. I have a doctorate in physics, sub-atomic physics. I worked with bubble chambers and particle accelerators. My profession is as a photographer and a publisher. The other important fact you need to know about me is that I was born non-labor cesarean, in 1942. So I know about cesarean birth from the child's point of view. Except for my own book, *Different Doorway*, there are no books that I know of on the child's experience of being born without the universal initiation of the trip down the birth canal, a trip that all vaginally born people take for granted. (It was noted here that in the large lecture hall there was only one other cesarean born person!!!) So I am the voice from the inside; you are all looking from the outside.

Working with cesarean birth was not really what I planned to do with my life. It evolved out of my own journey, out of dreams and out of trying to understand some of my personal and inter-personal difficulties. I lived at Esalen Institute in Big Sur, California for a year (1974-1975) and allowed images and emotions to emerge from within myself. A couple of years after that I worked extensively with Stanislav and Christina Grof, who helped me through this process. Stan, as many of you know, has made a wonderful map of vaginal birth, and a beautiful slide show of traditional art and art from his various patients. I looked at his map and thought, "Wonderful map, but it does not fit my territory." All the way through his 4-hour long slide show I had mixed feelings, fascination and feeling left out. So I made my own map.

We who are cesarean born are the beginning of technologically assisted birth. Use of *in vitro* fertilization, surrogate mothers, and all the different technologies are changing the traditional sequence and meaning of conception, labor and delivery. In the years to come, there will be people like me standing up and telling what it is like to be conceived *in vitro*. We whose births were technologically assisted tell about not only our own way of being born, we tell you, by contrast, something about the traditional birth. For instance, I have been able to verbalize much of what goes on in labor because I have had to learn it piece by piece, from the outside. With my not having had children and being born non-labor cesarean, my body has never experienced labor, either coming or going. I arrived here without having gone through the usual initiation of labor.

I think there is a great deal one learns in the journey down the birth canal. The stories of the vaginally born are all around us in the mythologies and artwork of many cultures. I am beginning to collect the mythology of the cesarean born.

It is unfortunate that little attention is paid to the difference between labor cesarean and non-labor cesarean. I coined the phrase non-labor cesarean, and it makes me happy to see it begin to appear in other places. From the child's point of view just sitting there and then suddenly being out is quite different from going through a long hard labor and then being pulled back out through the mother's abdomen. It is a very different dynamic.

For the labor cesarean, take some of the vaginal birth patterns Stan Grof has talked about, and some of the non-labor cesarean patterns I talk about, and each labor cesarean person can pick and choose what fits them, weave their own story. There may also be things that are unique to labor cesareans.

Going beyond a psychological perspective and using an anthropological perspective, I think of cesarean birth as creating a different native culture, native in the literal sense of having to do with birth.

In this talk today I am going to go through the four perspectives in the chart. This is a theoretical overview. I will use this framework to discuss some of the ways I have looked at cesarean birth. I will give particulars for each of the stages.

Thesis

This is the easy place to start. Here we look through the lens of cause and effect, traditional science. The question with which I started my journey was, "What are the effects of being born cesarean?" As a scientist, that was the obvious question for me to ask.

In broad terms a non-labor cesarean birth creates a different view of space and of time. Here I mean space in terms of our personal boundaries, our psychological boundaries, our emotional boundaries. In a workshop given by William Emerson, we did an exercise to find out where we felt a need to stop when we walk up to a person. Several people in the workshop walked right up and bumped into me without feeling that stopping place. William said that my boundaries were different, that everyone in the room was already inside my boundaries, that my boundaries were way out. That was helpful to me; it helped me understand some of my interpersonal misadventures. I had been letting too much in. I think one of the things vaginally born people learn in labor is a sense of "this much and no more." Non-labor cesarean people tend to let everything in. This is both a gift and a problem.

As for time, non-labor cesarean birth takes only about two minutes. In my own journey I came to realize that I felt a deep sense of panic if I couldn't complete something quickly and all in one movement. Deep down I felt I was not allowed to take a rest and leave something part way done. My survival programming was that that wouldn't work; you have to do it all at once or it doesn't count. A teenage friend recently said to me, "You know, Jane, when you decide to do something you give it all of your energy and you just really do it." That's a good description of the cesarean pattern; to either hold back timidly or be totally involved. It has been wonderful to learn from my vaginally born friends that it really is OK to do a bit then take a break, like the rhythms of labor. You do a bit, then rest, do more, rest, and so on.

A vaginally born person is on a positive trajectory when they are born. Things are getting better when they arrive. For a non-labor cesarean things are going along OK, the anaesthesia hits, then everything disintegrates just as they are delivered.

One of the gifts for a cesarean born is the ability to get from here to there quickly by enlisting the support of a group of helpers. At a cesarean birth there is a group of highly skilled people each doing their job, and the incredible transition of birth is thereby made rapidly. The ability to not have to struggle, to not have to labor every time you make a transition is a gift that cesarean born people bring to the world.

A cesarean born who is identified with her own way and looks at a vaginally born, she sees that they have a lot in common, but there are pieces that the vaginally born people don't seem to recognize. There is a part that the vaginally born people seem to ignore. If a vaginally born looks at a cesarean born there is a similar thing. "You are sort of like me but you seem like there is something you don't understand. What is the matter with you. You don't know how to relate in the way people are supposed to know how to relate." But when we get to fully appreciating our differences and not identifying with our own form, what we end up with is something that is larger than either of us. So the cesarean born brings gifts as well as difficulties, and the same for the vaginally born.

As for research on this topic, there is very little done. One woman did a master's thesis at Smith College. She asked certain questions of 25 vaginally born women and 25 cesarean born women and came up with some differences. One of them was that most of the cesareans had been fired from jobs somewhere along the way, and none of the vaginally born had. Being fired, like cesarean birth, is a sudden involuntary transition. But her sample was small and the experiment was not double blind.

Some of the reasons I think this research has not been done are:

1) It is cross-disciplinary and it does not fit into an academic category for which funding is available.

2) The idea that birth has anything to do with personality is only recently beginning to be widely accepted

3) It is hard to design appropriate research questions because the differences are at a deep level. I believe many orthodox research protocols make assumptions that are based on a vaginal birth worldview. They don't ask the right questions. For instance, double blind protocols assume a degree of separation between researcher and subject that may not be accurate for cesarean born people with their expanded sense of boundaries. One has to consider things like parapsychology; there are ways to know what is in a sealed envelope. With expanded consciousness one can do that. The ancient shamans knew this. So the whole double-blind protocol has its limitations. It assumes that we are separate individuals. Perhaps that deep sense of distinctness is one of the things learned in vaginal birth.

Antithesis

Here we still use cause and effect, but turned around. Instead of asking, "What are the effects of being born cesarean?" we ask, "What are some of its causes? What are the soul intentions, what are the karmic patterns that best find expression in a cesarean birth. For me this perspective was important because in dreams and in therapy work I had several apparent past life memories.

An example of this was a sense of having been the subject in an Aztec sacrifice. I found myself wondering to what extent a cesarean birth is a resonance of Aztec sacrifice. In both there is a person who is drugged, surrounded by a group of people, under a bright light, and cut open, then something precious is lifted up into the light. In a cesarean there is a birth; in the Aztec ritual there is a death. Perhaps the epidemic of cesarean births is all the Aztec victims coming back to heal themselves!

Synthesis

What became deeper truth for me was to step out of cause and effect totally. What mattered was the kind of response I got from cesarean people and from their mothers. I saw that deep acceptance of how things actually had been at birth is itself healing, and allows one to live more fully, to move on and not worry about cause and effect.

In this synthesis, I take my ideas about cesarean personality not as something to be scientifically proved or disproved, but as useful tools for transformation. It is clear to me that they are useful tools. One non-labor cesarean born woman, who has been a yoga teacher for 25 years, said she knew all this in her body, but my book gave her the words.

What I have done so far with cesarean birth exploration is not scientific research. I struggled with that, criticizing myself for being too subjective. But the thing that has kept me going these 22 years of exploring has been the reactions from other cesarean born people, especially when I speak of the boundaries and the relationship patterns. They start finishing sentences for me, and they say things like, "Yeah, I'm like that too. You mean I'm not crazy?" There are heartfelt reactions. And there are times when I talk with cesarean mothers and tell them that perhaps they are still laboring with their children. I see their eyes light up as they understand the intensity of the relationship with their child. They had been judging themselves and their children for having very intense encounters. I tell them it's labor!

In both the antithesis and the synthesis, we move beyond orthodox science. In his *Pre and Perinatal Psychology Journal* article "Expanding the Boundaries of Memory", David Chamberlain says, "Part of personal consciousness is alive and well outside the physical body." For me, making this step outside the usual boundaries of science was facilitated by something I first met *within* science. In sub-atomic physics, particle physics, and quantum mechanics I was faced with the breakdown of the idea of separate objects interacting. As an undergraduate I remember being told something like, "Light is a wave. Light is a particle. Both and neither at the same time." This apparent paradox (see the chapter "Science and Transformation") resolved itself for me fifteen years later in a transcendent, unitive experience in which neither "I" nor external objects existed separately. This leads to the fourth perspective.

Transcendence

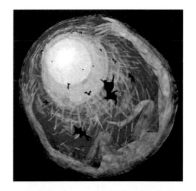

Words separate, divide and categorize but there is a reality beyond words. This is an experience of underlying unity, even beyond the idea of connection, which requires there be separate things to be connected!

Images are still apparently separate objects, but they can point to the unity. The upper painting is of falling into physical form; the lower one is of rising out of physical form, rejoining the light.

Birth, both cesarean and vaginal, is spirit coming into form, taking on limitation. Limits are good, boundaries are good. They make the dance that we enjoy as life. Death is the releasing, going back. The art is to learn how to journey back and forth through this tunnel, which is not necessarily the birth canal. I haven't been through the birth canal, yet these tunnel images come to me. I think of birth trauma memories as demons that guard this opening between the mundane and spirit.

Looking back, scientific causality was my starting point. I moved through a polarity with that reversed, then to a synthesis of these, then to an ability to move beyond. These are all stances that I have experienced during my journey, and are all useful at appropriate moments. No one is better than the others. They all have shadow sides that are distortions. Mastery comes in taking each stance appropriately.

See the "Cesarean Voices" website at www.eheart.com/cesarean/ for a collection of writings and artwork by cesarean-born people, parents, doctors, psychologists and birth professionals.

VISION CYCLE

This cycle of 24 paintings was inspired by a half-hour long visionary experience one evening in July 1977. Before it I had done an hour of yoga, then some sitting meditation. I followed awareness of body sensations and came to a state of simple acceptance, letting the day's experiences die, though noting flickers of fear in this dying.

I did the paintings a few at a time, not always in sequence, between July 1977 and March 1979. I needed time to grow and to integrate different parts of the vision before I could externalize them, ground them in the physical form of the paintings. The process of painting was itself part of my understanding and integrating what I had experienced in the vision. The paintings were done in opaque watercolor; each one is about nine inches wide. (See p. 86 for more on the painting process.)

The cycle is one turn on a spiral. I returned to where I started, but returned changed, moved to a new level of awareness. The cycle of paintings parallels the cycle of movement through my natal chart. When I first saw this correspondence I was astounded at the correlations between the paintings and the signs, planets, and houses in the chart shown in the diagram to the right. The connections to Huichol Indian shamanic cosmology came several months *after* the experience.

I experience the cycle as a map and a guide, a set of symbols to use as a tool for expansion of self-awareness. It is my personal mandala. My understanding of the initial visionary experience and the images from it continues to grow. I journey round and round the cycle. I even made myself a small set of cards, photographs of the paintings, that I use as an oracle to mirror my current inner state. It is a real delight to have a home-grown oracle!

The symbols are also more than just my personal images; they are archetypal images and can have meaning for the cycle of your journey too. Go through the paintings on the following pages several times, sometimes focusing on the flow of images and reading only the brief words in italic. Notice your mental, emotional, intuitive and physical responses to them. For you, your own experience is more important than what mine was. At other times enjoy reading the more detailed text and make your own interpretations as well.

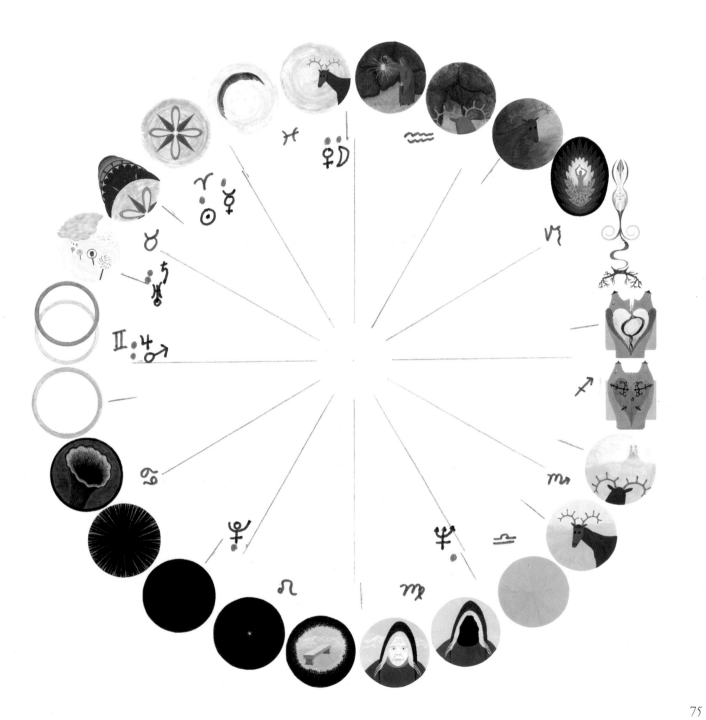

No wants ~ Stillness ~ Being

This after yoga and meditation. Silver symbolizes quiet receptivity.
Astrology: First house is "I am", being.

Orange flower ~ darkness in center. The way in, literally.
I choose to enter the darkness.

Having recently read about the value of going into the darkness
when at an impasse, I was aware of the dark center as an opportunity, a doorway into other realms, what the Huichol Indians call a
"nierika."

Into the darkness. No sense of confinement, rather one of great space.

Darkness - total - nothing else can be said about it.

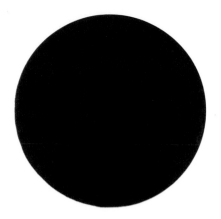

The most still darkness I have ever experienced. Not negative, not positive. Even these words and images are too explicit for this experience.
Astrology: Pluto is the farthest planet from the sun.

In the center of the darkness appear sharp crystal fragments of blue-white light, increasing in number and intensity. Cold icy land. Looking "back" into the darkness to see if the orange flower is visible. It is not. No way to go back.

Bench of blue ice in the icy land. Accepting this as my reality for now. No emotion. Only curiosity as to what will happen next, if anything.

Dual awareness of sitting on my meditation bench and on this inner bench. Very cold. Body shivers. Feeling like a tourist in a strange land.

Even during the experience I was aware that the bench was like an ice version of the granite benches on the common in the small New England town where I grew up.
Astrology: The nadir - the underworld.

A hag appears, black cape and head, gnarled face, intense blue eyes. She walks toward me. I wonder what this is all about, aware it is a test of some sort. Then I meet her face to face. I could get scared, but I don't. Very present and centered.

I wondered if I was "making up" these images - this seemed like a caricature of what I was "supposed" to meet in the underworld. She had a face that is mine, my mother's, my father's, my grandmother's, all in one. An image of personal history. All my fears.
Astrology: Fourth house is family and home.

Meeting her head on I ask, "Who are you?" She begins to dissolve. The face becomes darkness, a deep hole into nothingness.

The partly dissolved image is a dark ghost. It mirrors non-being to ego-me, to my small self. The darkness is another nierika.

Then the whole face dissolves and I find myself sitting again on the bench.

Astrology: Neptune is the dissolver.

At some time while I was on the bench, before or after the hag, I opened my eyes and returned to awareness of my room, but this did not feel comfortable. The cold icy feeling was still there and I knew I had to go back into the icy land for a while.

From the right a hooded reindeer appears, brown with fuzzy antlers. Its eyes are the same deep darkness, but the overall presence feels very friendly.

I was puzzled as to how to deal with this being. "Who are you?" didn't seem appropriate. The eyes are another nierika leading to yet another level.

While wondering how to relate to the deer, I see off in the distance a castle on a hill. Looking back at the deer I ask, "Are you supposed to take me there?" The answer was a wordless, "Yes."

"Kayumari" the deer is a Huichol spirit-guide. Delighted, I rode him toward the castle. Movement at last after so much stillness and confrontation. Going toward the sky-realm. The castle is its gateway, another nierika.

At the castle. It now bulges, and the door is like a heart. A lot of energy is moving in my body, changes in breathing.

A pregnant mother castle. I lost awareness of the deer-guide here and became entranced with the images and the physical experience. Fire in the upper windows is a clue to what is to follow.

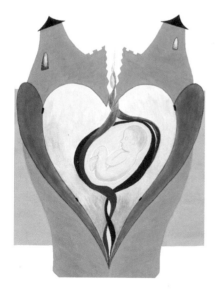

The doors fly open and I see myself as a baby - very clearly it is me. Black., green, blue and yellow curving shapes around the baby. Regressing into being the baby. Aware I am losing myself by letting this happen.

By now the experience was much more than visual and was moving very fast. Feelings and emotions moved through me. Memory of the experience is not as clear here.
Clearly the experience of birth. I was born non-labor cesarean so the upward, sudden birth is appropriate.

Baby flesh becoming adult female flesh. Much energy moving through my body. I see/feel energy curl from around the breasts up into the face. Flowers budding and opening. Chaos of organic forms. An explosion of growth. Face dissolves into an organic form, a large bud unfolding, moving, colors streaming.

This painting and the next are not exact representations of the visual part of the original experience. By this time it was much more than visual. These are attempts to put into visual form some of the quality of the overall experience,

Fire! All fire. Becoming fire. Grainy cellular reality.

Feeling as if I am falling over backwards off my wooden meditation bench. I am going crazy. I am dying. If I go into the white light I won't know how to return. Terror.

Wishing I had with me a human guide I trust. Energy streaming through body – I forget the specifics. Then I ask aloud, "What is this?" The intensity diminishes and I become aware of being present in my room. I open my eyes.

This seems to be the place from which ego-death and transcendence are possible. The place to get off the wheel of life. I wasn't ready! *Astrology:* Eighth house is the place of death and rebirth.

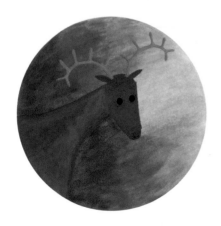

Eyes open, still aware of some fire. Tension in throat and mouth. Not satisfied with the present, feeling I have lost something precious. Wanting to return to the vision world, I close my eyes and immediately meet the deer again. Relief. I am ready to stay with my guide now. Trusting him. A friend.

The difficulties I had just encountered seem to have come from my having lost contact with the guide, from having identified with the forms that were disintegrating rather than with the transpersonal witness.

Telling the deer that I'm ready to go wherever I need to go now, we ride to a cave in some dark mountains. Deep terror, not fiery terror as before, more a sense of foreboding. Trusting the deer and staying in contact with him.

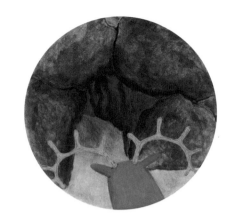

An old person holding a lamp giving off curved streamers of liquid light. I feel tempted to go into the light, to lose myself in vision. I hesitate when I hear an inner voice say, "It's important to remember that I am in a body." I sense that I have passed a test.

Immediately I am with the deer again. I want to remember these experiences, but know attachment will stop the process. I choose to let go in order to move on. The deer assures me it can lead me back to the memory of each part. I believe him and say, "OK, where to now?"

Astrology: The deer spirit guide was with me through the part of the cycle that corresponds to the fifth through ninth houses of my astrological chart, the big space where I have no planets.

I surrender to wherever he will take me next. Instead of being taken somewhere, I feel a sense of "circleness," of coming around, of return. A circle begins to appear.

Astrology: Moon and Venus - a beautiful crescent shape

The circle becomes the most beautiful mandala I have ever seen. I become entranced with its perfection. Then I notice that it is just an image; it is static. I let go of it, totally.

For a long time I couldn't paint this one because I had let go so totally and had forgotten the image. This is not the mandala I saw, but is one that, while I sketched it as part of another drawing, suddenly seemed adequate for this position in the cycle.
Astrology: The Sun is the energy source, is like a mandala.

Immediately after letting go, I am in a snowstorm of mandalas, each one perfect. I resist holding onto memory of any of them.

The blizzard of mandalas was much less orderly than this painting.

Then the mandalas become lollipops, and an angry voice from a dark cloud says, "You didn't grab on!" It has been trying to tempt me with images the way it would a little girl with a lollipop.

Humor at last after all the intensity! I hadn't become attached to the stillness, the flower, the darkness, the cold, the fear, the dissolution, the guide, baby-me, female-me, the white light, the liquid light, perfect form, or the lollipops.

Astrology: Saturn - form, limitation, and attachment followed immediately by Uranus - breaking free, the cosmic joker.

I relax and realize I have been in the land of the dead and had, even there, managed to stay in touch with life. My eyes open spontaneously. I am very present and more myself than I have ever felt. Seeing equally with both eyes, I am content, awed, peaceful, awake, and alive.

Gold now as well as silver. Silver refined by the fire of experience. The dynamic in harmony with the receptive.

* * * * * * *

Sitting for a while I was aware of easy access to both worlds — inner and outer. I had crossed the line easily several times during the journey. I felt much gratitude to all my teachers for the experience and knowledge that enabled me to journey safely.

Then began the rest of my life! I ran though the whole journey in memory, with a moment of feeling I had finally fallen for the trap of attachment by trying to recall the experience. But what is life but the ebb and flow of attachment and release, of inbreath and outbreath! So I surrendered once again, this time *to* form. That evening I began writing and the following morning began to paint.

An experience like this is a challenge - work is required to bring it more fully into the ordinary waking world and to learn from it. The following are notes I made on the process of doing the paintings.

October 16, 1977

The bulging castle had enough charge around it for me that I did a pencil sketch of it the next day. Then the following day I did the orange flower. I didn't remember any background color from the vision, but during painting an intuition of maroon emerged. It felt right — some later connection with orange and maroon being the colors of the robes of Tibetan Buddhist monks.

The bench was next. I felt quite intensely the coldness, aloneness and desolation of that place as I painted. I also felt a lot of energy and excitement.

I first sketched the hag as she walked toward me, but that didn't feel right. She seemed like a cartoon and didn't have the energy of the experience. I then did a quick sketch of the hag dissolving and was pleased and amazed at the power of the stylized image that emerged. Painting it I felt I was entering an even colder more dead place. I was uncomfortable with and even a bit shaken by the painting after I finished it.

Then somehow I got the idea to start immediately on the deer even though I was tired of painting. Just sketching the deer changed my energy completely and brought much relief. While I painted the deer I felt it was a friendly, positive presence and enjoyed being with it. This was a comfortable interlude before the journey continued.

At this point I laid these first four paintings out on the table and became aware of a too sudden transition between the flower and the bench. Something was missing. So I did the totally black painting and liked what it did to the sequence, separating the warm energy of the flower from the cold icy underworld.

Doing the painting of riding the deer toward the castle I was aware of whole new element in the process. Movement had entered. The first five images I had painted had been rather static; they are confrontations of various sorts. Riding the deer I began to move. Hope, excitement and anticipation

were all present. The warm friendly energy of the deer took on a more dynamic quality in the light around the castle. I found myself singing and dancing after completing this painting.

While painting the castle with the heart-shaped door I was aware of much blocked energy. Tremendous tension in me. I got quite sick the day after finishing it.

Painting the opened castle was straight-forward until I got to the baby. Then I realized I'd never really let myself look at babies clearly. I felt awe and wonder as I touched the form with my brush. While painting the spirals I felt a rising and opening within me. At first the castle windows were pale yellow, but that seemed not quite right. Adding the intensity of the red and orange pointed to the energy still locked up in the castle. The baby is not the end of the process.

The process of painting the female form with energy channels was different, not so true to the visual component of the original experience, though parts of it are what I saw - the curling energy arising from the breasts and the bud form with fire at the top. I started from the bottom with the roots. It was the first day of my period and I felt very much in touch with my pelvis. After painting that part I lay down and listened to music and let energy flow. I felt the sadness of having a barren womb. Then the experience changed and I transcended identifying with being either mother or child. With this came a sense of relief and freedom. The next part, the curving green form did not have a lot of emotional charge. The curling form around the breasts I first did in gold, but that didn't seem right. When I closed my eyes and relaxed, my whole visual field turned to deep pink—raspberry sherbet and good tastes!. So I painted it pink.

The crystal star I associate with the third chakra, the center of power. The painting seemed to gain cohesion. The opening in the throat is vocal expression; it connects with an area of tension for me. The face was hard to paint. The pink in the mouth connects with the breasts. The eyes were those same disturbing blue eyes, like the hag's. I alternated painting them open and then closed and again open. I felt good painting the purple, gold, red, orange and yellow part at the top. The last parts I painted were the red dot in the forehead and the blue moving into the cheeks. Both grew out of sensations in my face. By the time I did the blue I was getting impatient and it shows. I was eager to finish this painting project that had possessed me all summer.

Notes on four additional paintings - October 31, 1977

The streaks of orange going into darkness were easy to paint. This is the abstract, purely visual, part of the experience. This painting makes clearer the transition from the flower to the darkness

It was possible to paint the image of the hag's face only after I processed and met some of my fears associated with intense blue eyes.

The plain blue painting expressed the pause between the hag and the deer, the time of again just being in the icy cold place.

The painting of the fire image brought a sense of completion and acceptance of having refused the white light. The process of doing the paintings stopped here - for a while!

Painting again - January 8, 1978 - rainy and windy day

Last Sunday I was feeling really low, despairing. I took an afternoon nap hoping for a dream that might provide some guidance. I received the following dream:

Walking out through the orchard at my childhood home I meet a friend who seems very energized, glowing. She tells me of a dead deer she has seen out further in the pasture and woods. It has large antlers. She tells me that if I am up to it, it would be good for me to drag it back to the house. She starts giving me directions on how to find it, then seeing I don't understand she says she will go with me.

We arrive at the deer. It is dead but does not seem yucky. It feels like a mix of an actual dead deer she and I had seen once on a walk, and the deer in my painting. I feel glad to be in its presence.

I awoke soon after this.

That night I had a hard time sleeping. Lying there I realized I needed to continue the paintings. I knew that the paintings would only be a representation of the experience, yet it seemed right to go ahead and do them -- and let them "do"me!

The next morning I got a sense of the paintings being in a circle, not in a linear series. I sketched them in a circle and felt a sense of returning home. I saw the vision, and the paintings, as one turn on a spiral, a return to the starting place but on a new level.

For four days I had a good rhythm of painting in the morning and doing yard work for a friend in the afternoon. I first painted the second deer painting. Good to be back with my friend and guide.

Painting both of the cave paintings was a struggle. I felt that dark place within myself. It was good to do ordinary work in the sunny afternoons. The fifth morning I planned to paint the mandala, but I felt much resistance. I did a sketch with marking pens but it felt stiff and uninspired. Then I thought, "That's it for painting for now." So mysterious is this process, starting and stopping as I grow into being able to assimilate parts of the vision experience, then become saturated and burned out and need to stop. I wonder when the process will resume.

Spring 1979

I was able to complete the cycle of paintings after seeing that a small mandala I had painted as part of a larger work would fit as the mandala in this cycle, even though it was not the original mandala I had seen then totally released.

I realized recently that at the castle I lost contact with the deer. That is why I got so scared and out of control. I was trying to go through all that by myself, as my small self without the guidance of the inner shaman part of me. I was afraid of dying because I was identified with aspects of my personality, which actually were dying.

I just went back through the experience of approaching the castle on the deer and felt the energy of the castle, baby, woman and fire while still in the quiet witness presence of the deer. Last week a friend told me that for the Huichols the deer *is* the shaman, the one who can travel safely in subtle realms. That was a key to a missing piece of the puzzle for me.

SILO

One cool grey early October day in 1974 Gia-fu and I were walking on a gravel back road in northern Vermont. It would have been a gloomy day except that the fall foliage was in its prime. On that grey day the colored leaves were extra brilliant. Maybe they create a "da-glo" effect, with the invisible ultraviolet light that falls on them being absorbed and re-emitted at visible wavelengths so that at the red and orange wavelengths there is actually more light coming off the leaf than is falling onto it. It did seem that way to me.

Shortly after we turned up an even smaller dirt road we came to a no-longer-mowed field that had a few small bushes growing among the grass and gone-by flowers. In the middle of the field stood a most unique silo. It had been built log-cabin style from two-by-fours and had neat little dormer windows in its roof. The barn that had stood beside it

was long gone; only a hole in the ground and some granite foundation stones remained.

The silo seemed to defy time as it stood there long after the farm it served was gone and as the glorious colors signaled the bittersweet end of another season of growth. I have often wondered what hill farmer built this silo and how he would feel if he knew his creation had long out-lived the barn.

NATIVE IMAGES

I stood by the open window in my second floor bedroom at the back north side of the 1765 colonial New England house that was my childhood home and looked out across the fields to the woods beyond. I was probably about eight or ten years old. I held a carved stick to which I had attached ribbons and feathers. It was a special stick to me, though I could not have said why. It vaguely had something to do with what little I knew of Indians. I liked the stick, but it seemed not connected with the rest of what went on in my life in that small New England town north of Boston. I felt I couldn't tell anyone that it was special to me.

I always was attracted to Indian ways, or at least to what I thought were Indian ways. When we played cowboys and Indians, I always wanted to be an Indian; I made my own bows and arrow, and constructed small tipis from sheets and poles. My grandmother saved for me the "Straight Arrow Injunuity" cards that came in shredded wheat boxes. They had much information on Plains Indian crafts and lifestyle.

My best friend through grade school lived in an area that had in the past held Indian villages. Frequent discovery of arrowheads had led her grandfather to name his land Arrowhead Farm. Playing in those woods and fields we imagined—or felt!—the presence of Indians.

At some point my small staff got packed away and then discarded as I grew into the world of high school and college.

Looking back I think it was perhaps a shaman's staff, an object of the ordinary physical world that is useful in leading one's awareness beyond into more subtle realms.

At Arrowhead Farm

It was not until the 1970's that I again became actively interested in Indian things. While in one of Stan Grof's month-long workshops at Esalen Institute in Big Sur I met a white American who had trained for several years with a Huichol Indian shaman in Mexico. He led us in some ceremonies around a fire, and I immediately felt at home. A few

At the Sunflower Festival,
Colville Reservation, Omak WA 1978

years later I spent time with friends who worked at the school on an Indian reservation in north-central Washington state. There I got to know modern Indians and saw them as real people, not some idealized image in my mind.

While I lived in the San Francisco Bay Area in the early 1980's I was active in a group that was loosely affiliated with the Native American Church as well as with the Huichols. There were regular evenings of singing, drumming, and praying in a tipi around a fire, as well as occasional all night ceremonies led by various Native Americans.

During that time an ambivalence was growing in me. The ceremonies and practices felt good to me, but I was aware that as a white person I was sort of playing Indian. I didn't really belong to these traditions. I tried to be true to myself, though, and did not just cut myself off from all that Indian ways meant to me — a close connection to both earth and spirit.

Some Native Americans say that we white folks should look back to the indigenous spiritual traditions of our ancestors, to Celtic mythology for instance. But my ancestors came to this continent, to New England, eleven generations ago. So where do I fit? Of what land am I a native? It is hard to know. Sometimes I envy Native Americans who at least, in spite of the pain and dislocations, have memory of an intact native tradition. For me that is all gone. Maybe this connection is what I was longing for as a child playing Indian and holding my colorful staff.

During the early 1980's I was also pursuing my explorations of what it meant to have been born cesarean. I came to see that to really understand birth, one needs to look at the larger picture of what it is for a soul to come into physical form. So I began taking workshops on core shamanic practice from Michael Harner, culminating with an intensive month-long experience at Esalen in 1984. His work as an anthropologist had led him to see certain practices that were common to many indigenous cultures around the world. We learned shamanic practice, but without cultural trappings. I got the tools I needed for inner journeying, though after the workshop I felt a lack of community into which to ground the practices.

Shortly afterwards, I saw an ad for a used tipi for sale and met with the man selling it who was part Native American. He seemed to think that I would take good care of his lodge and sold it to me. I then embarked in the very labor intensive task of making a set of 17 twenty-five foot poles for the tipi. We set up the tipi in the back field of a friend who lived near me in Point Reyes Station, CA. We used the tipi for personal shamanic journeying and for occasional meetings of the classes my friend taught on shamanic art.

During this time I often made moccasins, both for myself and for friends, vaguely aware that my intention was to help people walk softly on the earth.

Moccasins I made for my twin niece and nephew when they were born in 1986.

Rainbow Fire
canvas 6 feet diameter

I made this to create the experience of diverse people sitting together around a fire without actually using a fire. It was used in schools, homes and even in a tipi during daytime.

I also made for myself a water drum, a deeply resonant drum made from a three-legged cast iron pot with water in it and a skin tied across the top.

With Teles, about 1983

This brought me to some good discussions with Native American ceremonial leaders as to just what I was doing with such a drum. By staying true to myself and with the support of some dreams, I came to see that I was being inspired by native ways but not exactly copying them. I felt especially good about the path I was on after one group evening of drumming, singing and praying in a tipi during which Teles Goodmorning from the Taos Pueblo used my drum the whole time.

When I moved to Mount Shasta, CA in 1987, I bought a new tipi and set it up in my yard. It has been a guest bedroom, a place for singing and praying, a place for neighborhood home-schoolers to meet while doing a unit on Indians, and a place for wonderful marshmallow roasts. The first time we did marshmallows I felt a bit irreverent, but soon saw it as just another kind of ceremony!

One morning recently I was thinking about my relation to Native American ways. It was easy to slip into feeling like a guilty white honky. After all, it was people of my race who raped the land, the people and the culture of the Native Americans. The whites had totally different values and imposed them on the natives and the land. I tried to feel what this had been like for the Native Americans.

Then the phone rang. A friend told me of making a lot of money on an obscure computer stock in the stock market the day before. "Sure beats working," he said. Then I realized I did know some of what it must have felt like to be a Native American 100 years ago. The values of the culture of material greed threaten to sweep away what I know and value just as much as the miners and ranchers of the 1800's destroyed the native culture with its values. In a way, all of us who value integrity, respect for the Earth and connection to spirit are in much the same position as the Native Americans.

All through these past 20 years I have worked with my ambivalence about Native American ways. There was much in them that fed my soul, yet I did not want to be disrespectful of traditional culture. I began to look for the essence of what I am attracted to and tried to find ways to touch those same places within my own culture.

In 1997 I finished training as hot-air balloon pilot, earned my commercial pilot certificate and bought a used balloon, which I named "Dragon Egg." Floating over the land made me wonder if ballooning was an experience similar to that of astronauts on space walks. Another balloon pilot had a former astronaut as a passenger. The astronaut confirmed my thoughts, saying that a balloon flight was the closest he had ever come to the space walk experience since coming back from space.

I find that flying brings me to many of the same places as the native practices. A balloon flight can be much like a ceremony. There is preparation, the flight, cleaning up and sharing food afterward. And it seems to transform people. I find myself smiling the rest of the day after I fly in the morning. Like native ceremonies it can give one perspective on ordinary daily life. I am delighted at last to find a practice that is rooted right in my own native culture.

Dragon Egg in Shasta Valley
with Mount Shasta and the Shasta River

At the Indigenous
Environmental
Network conference

Then this summer, in 1998, I was invited to bring my balloon to an indigenous environmental gathering, a meeting of native people from all over the globe, including many Native Americans. We did an evening of brief tethered rides for the winners of a raffle that raised funds for protection of traditional sacred sites. The next morning, as at the other end of the encampment the sacred fire for a sweat lodge blazed up in the morning twilight, we again inflated the balloon, its own fire glowing in the pre-dawn light! Our sunrise flight with some of the Native Americans was exquisite. We flew over the woods and fields with Mount Shasta in the distance. I had come full circle, bringing my own native practice back to people whose native practices had shown me the way over the years.

And, after all, all of us are natives, natives of Earth!

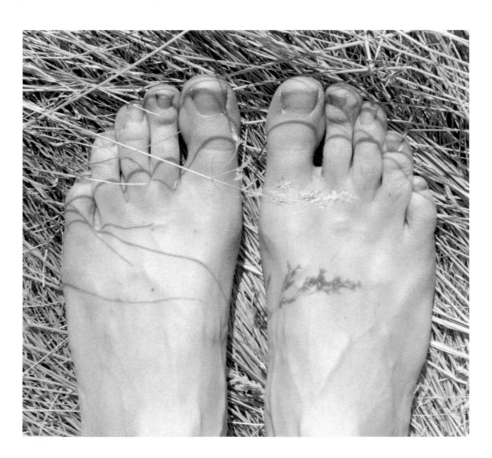

SCIENCE AND TRANSFORMATION
Levels of Reality in Science and in Consciousness

It is easy to blame science and technology for the environmental problems in which we now find ourselves. We imagine that if we could just go back to nature, everything would be all right. But that is not possible. What is possible, however, is for the person using a technology to do so with a state of awareness that is appropriate to it. My training in physics and my subsequent explorations of consciousness have led me to believe that this might not only solve our problems, but also facilitate the evolution of our consciousness. The "problems" may actually be opportunities for growth!

In this article I focus on nuclear technology and quantum physics because of my experience in that area, but the point I make generalizes to all areas of science and technology.

The technological success of science has brought such change and such improvement in living conditions in the past 300 years that we have tended to accept as absolutely real the rather limited concepts and worldview on which it is based. These ideas influence our perceptions, actions, and how we give form to our experience.

Among the early Greeks, "physis," the word from which "physics" was derived, was the study of the nature of reality, the inner reality of human consciousness as well as that of external matter. But over the past 300 years changes in consciousness have lagged far behind the theoretical and technical changes. For example, we are using the powerful tools of atomic physics with a consciousness rooted in the older, mechanistic Newtonian physics.

What is the history of the relationship between scientific theory and direct personal experience, and how is this relationship evolving?

The alchemists, whose work preceded modern experimental science, acted from a union of inner and outer experience. The processes that occurred in their furnaces and crucibles and the processes that occurred in their bodies and consciousness were two aspects of the same reality. To speak of one was to speak of the other.

In the 1600's, partly in reaction to the witch hunts connected with misuses of the occult, Newtonian physics was created with its emphasis on objective measurement. Great effort was made to remove the "contamination" of subjective experience from scientific work. Scientists lost touch with the mystical aspect of their work and instead came to value the ability to predict and control the material world. Analytical and separative thinking is ideal for this pursuit and has deeply affected how most of us see reality, people as well as things. But even in Newtonian physics there is some connection to direct experience. Concepts such as tension, force, and pressure appeal to a muscular common sense, and the theoretical models are easily visualized. These theories make sense, literally! They are rooted in sensory experience.

Electromagnetic theory of the late 1800's represented a step away from direct experience. It speaks of electromagnetic waves moving through a vacuum, waves where there is nothing that is waving! For most of us this doesn't make sense, and physicists of the late 1800's made great but unsuccessful efforts to retain in the theory an ether that fills space and carries electromagnetic waves just as water carries water waves. It was hard to give up the connection with direct sensory experience.

With the quantum physics of the 1920's things got worse. Now there were no consistent models that could be visualized or connected to sensory experience in any way. All attempts at making models led to paradoxes. Quantum physics was an abstract mathematical formalism, and it worked! It gave numbers that agreed with measurement, and it predicted new phenomena that were subsequently observed. As physics students we were told that all attempts to connect quantum physics with our direct experience were irrelevant, and that we should ignore the confusion that we felt when faced with a reality that seemed unreal.

For me, this confusion was the starting point of a long journey that has led me to an understanding of the mismatch between the technology we use and the consciousness with which we use it. Noticing the parallels between the paradoxes of quantum physics and the paradoxes of Zen Buddhism, I made intellectual explorations of oriental philosophy and religion. Dissatisfied with purely intellectual explanations, I turned to meditation and to the experiential aspects of humanistic and transpersonal psychology. For a while, the confusion only increased, but then, about 15 years after I first encountered it, one of the paradoxes of quantum physics, the wave/particle paradox, was resolved for me in a spontaneous transcendent experience. The wave/particle paradox says, "Light is a wave spread out in space. Light is point particles taking up no space at all. Both of these and neither of these all at once." During the transcendent experience I realized that the wave/particle paradox had functioned as a koan for me, as a riddle that had led me to a new state of consciousness.

This happened during the time I was participating in a sensory awareness study group. One afternoon I sat on a couch by a window reading Fritjof Capra's *Tao of Physics*. His ideas were not new to me, and it was with delight and interest that I was reading his book in its final form. I was reading the chapter entitled "Beyond Language" where he speaks of the paradoxical nature of mystical experience, of Zen koans, and of how through their lack of logic koans lead one to experience a reality that is beyond language. He compared this to the experience of the physicists who invented quantum physics:

> "Here we find a striking parallel to the paradoxical situation which confronted physicists at the beginning of atomic physics. As in Zen, the truth was hidden in paradoxes that could not be solved by logical reasoning, but had to be understood in terms of a new awareness; the awareness of atomic reality. The teacher here was, of course, nature, who like the Zen masters does not provide any statements. She just provides the riddles." — F. Capra, *The Tao of Physics*, p.49

The phrase "awareness of atomic reality" triggered in me an experience that lasted about a half hour and was accompanied by changes that were noticed by people around me who commented that I seemed to be in a transcendent state. The experience began with a sense of sudden dissolution, especially of visual forms. The initial experience is impossible to describe in words. After a moment, I was aware of patterns of energy, millions of pinpoints of light, and a confused rush of visual sensation. Soon the experience stabilized somewhat, and I became aware of visual forms corresponding to what I now would call the furniture in the room and the sunlight on the trees outside. But everything was somehow different; there was no in-here/out-there split in my seeing!

This experience of no-separation cannot be fully described in words since words are, in their essence, distinctions and separations. It was an experience of union in which I and the world of objects did not exist separately. In this state of awareness there was no space or sense of separation between objects and my eyes. Thus I felt no need for light to exist to connect objects to eyes. Objects, eyes, and light no longer had the objective existence they had seemed to have just before. Separate self-identity and separate objects were optional ways of structuring experience rather than absolute realities. I wandered around delighted, awed, and amazed. I was aware that I had often had moments of this kind of seeing while looking through a camera. I had described it as "becoming what I photograph," even though that had then seemed crazy, impossible, and not quite accurate.

When experienced as two alternative ways of structuring awareness, rather than as qualities of something objectively real, the existence of light-as-waves and light-as-particles no longer seemed paradoxical. I realized that the wave/particle paradox had been my first koan, and that I had just solved it. The phrase "awareness of atomic reality" had pulled together my experiences in awareness work, in physics, and in photography to create a new state of awareness.

This new seeing gradually faded. I think that I was feeling overwhelmed and not ready to let go of my old worldview or of my separate identify. Since then, sometimes spontaneously and sometimes in meditation, I re-experience that seeing for short periods of time. I also find that I am more open to the possibility that things are not as they seem to be. I have learned to trust my experience of reality more than I trust what other people say about reality.

I had felt confused and had judged myself to be stupid when I first encountered the wave/particle paradox. I had accepted the orthodox physics thinking that says that quantum physics has no meaning for personal reality, that it is just a computational device, and that questions about things you can't measure are meaningless. I now look at the confusion as an opportunity for learning and growth rather than as an indication of my stupidity. The difficulties and confusion I experienced when I first studied quantum physics were not caused by quantum physics itself, but by the limited perspective I had and by my fear of letting go of this perspective. The following statements by physicist David Bohm were for me an affirmation of what I had experienced.

> "The typical reaction of a student who studies quantum mechanics is that first he doesn't understand it, and by a year or two later he says that there is nothing to understand because it is nothing but a system of computation. At the same time they've got to say, no, it isn't just that, we're discussing reality. After all, physicists would have no motive for the work they do if they didn't believe that these particles are really the building blocks of the universe. So, you see, you have to sustain this myth. It's actually not so easy. It takes several years and a lot of skill to train people to be able to do it (avoid the philosophical implications of quantum physics)."
>
> "Let's take a physicist. He's been subjected to all these courses in quantum mechanics and pressures to think in this way. He'll be approved of if he does, disapproved of if he doesn't, he gets a job if he does, not if he doesn't, and so on, and so on. The minute the idea occurs of thinking in another way, there will be intense pressure which will blot it out." -- D. Bohm, "The Enfolding-Unfolding Universe," *ReVision*, vol. I, #3/4, Summer/Fall 1978, pp. 31 & 36

The wave particle "koan" experience was for me the seed of a new understanding of the relationship between physics and direct experience. Science, which often seems to be an attempt to explain and use nature, is at its deepest level a search for meaning, not just intellectual understanding, but a direct knowing of reality. The strong desire for theories that make sense is an expression of this. There are, however, two aspects of making sense: 1) being sensory, and 2) having meaning or connection with direct experience. It is possible to give up the first without giving up the second. Physicists have generally assumed that human experience of the world must be sensory and that human consciousness follows the mechanistic laws of Newtonian physics. By denying, or simply being ignorant of, levels of reality and states of consciousness that go beyond sensory experience, physicists assume that it is necessary to give up the possibility of any direct experience of the reality that the mathematical theories of modern physics describe. All that is really necessary is giving up the requirement that this experience be in the ordinary sensory modes.

The transcendent experience that was facilitated by the wave/particle "koan" showed me that direct experience of the world of quantum physics is indeed possible, that quantum physics does have meaning. The confusion and paradoxes that emerge when one attempts to relate quantum physics to sensory experience resolve when the reality described by quantum physics is experienced directly. From that state of consciousness statements such as, "In quantum physics we cannot take ourselves out of the picture," "The observer has become the participator," and "There is no absolute truth out there." become descriptions of one's direct experience, not just descriptions of a physics theory.

We all have direct experience of the world of Newtonian physics. It makes sense to us, literally. And, as I have described, direct experience of the world of quantum physics is also possible. It was probably experienced by the inventors of quantum physics, and it is similar to meditative and mystical experiences described in many traditions. Also from experiences of my own and from accounts of other people's experiences it seems likely that it is also possible to experience directly the worlds of relativity theory, of electromagnetism, and of other parts of physics, and that many psychic and healing phenomena that appear extraordinary on our usual Newtonian, sensory reality are actually quite ordinary in these other realities.

I do not mean to imply that consciousness can in any way be explained by physics. Rather, I am simply saying that the correlation between the external world described by physics and the various kinds of direct experience of reality, the different levels of consciousness points to an interconnection between consciousness and matter. Neither one causes or explains the other. Both are aspects of the unnameable underlying unity that has been given many names including Tao, The One, God, and Self.

But why is it that the new physics which clearly has a potential for giving us a less separative view of reality, has instead been used mostly in very separative ways, e.g. building bombs, tearing up the land to mine uranium, and polluting the world with nuclear wastes? Why is there a mismatch between our technological development and the growth of our consciousness, our experience of reality? And what can be done to correct this imbalance?

One reason for the mismatch lies in the difficulty of translating quantum physics from mathematics into ordinary language. The people who design nuclear technology are engineers. Most of them make no pretense of having a deep philosophical understanding of physics. Only recently have a few people written non-technical books about quantum physics. Thus, only physicists had even the possibility of realizing that quantum physics has implications for consciousness. But because of their training in Newtonian physics, most physicists are not particularly open to experiencing these implications. Direct experience of the realms described by quantum physics is not easily available to people whose awareness has been limited by a Newtonian concept of reality (refer back to the second part of the Bohm quote above).

Another reason is that there seems to be a high priority in humans for our inner and outer realities to be congruent, to match and to support each other. And since most of us, including engineers and physicists, assume that human experience of the world must be sensory, there is great psychological pressure to try to reduce quantum physics to the level of the kind of experience we allow ourselves, the sensory, separative, Newtonian level.

Physicists studying quantum physics are faced with the choice of either 1) making paradoxical descriptions of the world of quantum physics in an attempt to have it make sense, to be sensory, or 2) declaring that quantum physics has no connection with direct experience. In scientific training the latter choice is stressed. At the time of learning quantum physics each physicist experiences the confusion mentioned earlier. It is a confusion that is not just intellectual; it involves the whole of one's being and challenges one's sensory, separative, Newtonian self-image and worldview. Then most physicists make the choice to suppress the confusion and disregard the conflict.

So we have produced several generations of scientists and engineers who are technically proficient in the use of nuclear technology and who have been taught to separate it from their inner personal experience, usually by denying or numbing awareness of the inner. This ensures the separative, insensitive, inhumane use of nuclear technology.

When we realize that it is the assumption of separation between ourselves and what we observe that is the root of this misuse, we can recognize the necessity of dealing with nuclear energy from the appropriate state of consciousness, from a directly experienced awareness of the interconnectedness of everything, of union with the universe. From this state of awareness nuclear bombs and nuclear pollution are unthinkable; one would experience them as suicide, as bombing and polluting one's self. This is a solution to the problem through transcendence or dissolution of it. The problem is no longer a problem because of a shift to a more expanded awareness, rather than because of a "fix-it" solution created on the same level of awareness in which the problem was stated. If in some way nuclear weapons were dismantled without this shift in awareness, our troubles would not be over, for the attachment to the separative consciousness would only emerge in another, perhaps worse, manifestation.

It is important to remember that it is not separative consciousness itself that is the problem here, but our clinging to it and use of it in inappropriate situations. Separative thinking and Newtonian mechanics are perfectly marvelous tools for mechanical situations, but not for the use of nuclear energy. (In fact, in the unitive state one does not even consider "using" something. There is nothing separate to be used!)

The unitive state of awareness is necessary not only for people who work with nuclear energy and technology, but also for the "anti-nuclear" people. Much anti-nuclear sentiment is just as separative and destructive as the force it opposes. The increasing use of non-violence training among anti-nuclear people is an encouraging step toward the recognition of this.

I will conclude with what might seem to be an amazing statement: I have not met anyone, not even a physicist and certainly not myself, who understands quantum physics with his or her whole being, with body, mind, and spirit. Some understand it functionally; they can put it to use to create new technology. Some understand it intellectually; they can use it to make predictions in particle physics. Some understand it philosophically; they can see parallels with oriental philosophies and religions as well as with many varieties of mysticism. Some people understand it intuitively; it seems to be an appropriate metaphor for experiences they have had in meditation. But I know no one for whom it is a living reality, for whom it makes sense at all levels of their being. Quantum physics may be a riddle that the universe has given us as a teacher. We are still learning its solution!

We are in a situation where we will either experience large scale evolution to planetary, unitive awareness or not survive. Every scientist who has studied quantum physics has been given a koan, a seed that if allowed to sprout could result in great unfolding and growth in awareness. The concepts of modern quantum physics are particularly powerful for us because they touch us deep within our existing scientific belief system rather than overlaying it with a set of beliefs from another culture.

The nuclear crisis is both a problem and an opportunity. Just as in many mythologies the demons guard a treasure, there is within the nuclear problem a jewel, a seed of transformation. The kind of action on the nuclear crisis that at this point seems appropriate is work on transforming consciousness, coupled with continued technological, political, social, ecological, and educational work done by people who know and experience unitive consciousness.

While this article has focused on quantum physics and the related nuclear technology, I feel sure that other areas of science and their related technologies also have within them similar seeds of transformation that will sprout and grow when we approach them with a willingness to learn and to be changed.

HERMAN'S GIFT

An hour ago Herman, one of my three cats, came in through the cat door with big thumping noises. He came into the living room all fluffed up and excited. I went to him, then saw lying on the laundry room floor a just dead young jack rabbit. A bit of its fur was stuck to its no longer seeing eye. It was a foot long nose to tail, nearly as big as the cat.

I picked it up — still warm — and carried it out the front door, spilling along the way a few big blots of dark red blood, echoing the equally dark red strawberries I had been eating on my cereal when the cat came in.

Once out the door, Herman seemed more interested in rubbing on me than in eating the rabbit. I guess in the cat world I am top cat in my house and he was bringing his catch to me as a gift.

So I got his sister Josephine off the bed where she was napping and showed her the rabbit out on the grass. She knew how to respond and took a few bites, but she soon gave up as it seemed that the fur was too thick and bothersome.

I got rubber gloves and a short sharp knife, and carried the body a ways away from the house — it was now a body, not a dead rabbit. Looking up into the foggy sunshine and the trees just sprouting leaves I found myself heartfully opening to that which is beyond naming.

I cut into the belly and pulled out the guts — stomach full of still green, chewed-up grass, gut progressing from brown slime to rabbit pellets. The place where vegetarian rabbit transmutes plants into rabbit body that supports rabbit consciousness and feeds carnivores, also into manure that feeds more plants.

Steam rose gently into the dewy morning air from the warm blood in the belly cavity.

Then I gave the rabbit back to the cats. Josie ate some of the liver and promptly barfed it out onto the grass. She went off and caught herself a bird — tasted better than rabbit, I guess.

Edmund, the third of my five-year-old litter-mate cats, then appeared and went right to work eating — like a small black panther cat with prey, nosing intently into the bloody open body of the rabbit. He ate for a while but also became frustrated with the fur.

I then skinned the rabbit, still awed and amazed at the transformations taking place as the body now became meat — much like chicken! As I cut the joints apart I was very aware that I was nowhere near as skilled as the cutter-of-meat mentioned in Chuang Tsu.

I gave Edmund a thigh joint which he chewed on for a while. I put the guts, skin, feet and ears out back in the bushes to feed wild animals less fussy than my well-fed domesticated cats. The carcass with kidneys, lungs, heart and liver still in it lay on the grass beside the head and what was left of the thighs.

I called a neighbor who has a dog. He came with a plastic bag for what remained of the jack rabbit's body.

We spoke of hunting — he did a bit years ago, and I went once with an old boyfriend shooting squirrels. We spoke of butchering — I grew up with chickens being killed often for dinner, with good anatomy lessons from Mother while we cleaned them. And he has raised many animals for food. Butchering always brings that sense of awe he says.

All through this I am so present — in body — aware of life — and of death.

Looking in the mirror I know the blood, bones, meat and sinews behind the skin of my face. Life is such a wondrous mystery. Herman really did bring me a gift this morning.

Edmund, earlier that same morning

INCARNATION

The dictionary defines *incarnate* as "invested with bodily, especially human, form and nature." It is derived from the Latin word "carn" meaning flesh or meat, as in "carnivore."

All of us here on the earth are incarnate. That much is simple. But our diverse philosophies, theologies, and worldviews give us widely varying attitudes toward the simple fact of incarnation. Take for example the abortion question. On one side are those who so value the tiniest bit of human incarnation that even very early abortion is seen as murder. On the other side are those who so value the freedom of an adult woman to live her own life and the right of all children to be truly wanted that they see abortion is an important option to preserve. Both sides have people willing to die for their views.

Since the late 1970's I have found myself in the fortunate position of knowing the possibility of going beyond the either-or, the *thesis-antithesis*, of this question, and even beyond the common *synthesis* of a ban on abortion combined with better adoption opportunities for the unwanted children. Given recent discoveries in the field of perinatal psychology about the trauma that adoption is for the child, even adoption into a loving family, this synthesis is not a real solution. It still compromises the experience of the child.

The *metathesis**, or transcendence, perspective on abortion came to me about 1977 when two women friends of mine happened to be visiting me in my apartment in Mendocino, CA at the same time. As I sat there listening they discovered that each of them had had an unwanted pregnancy, and both had come, in deep meditation and with a small supportive circles of friends, to what they felt was true communication with their unborn child. The women had communicated both their love for the child and the fact of not being able to give the child a good home, physically and emotionally, at that particular time. Each said they had felt their child understood and agreed to leave. Both women had had spontaneous miscarriages the following day.

*(see pp. 65-73 for discussion of *thesis, antithesis, synthesis* and *metathesis*.)

By transcending conventional assumptions about the nature of human identity, especially that of unborn children, these women had simultaneously been truly pro-choice, respecting their own needs, and truly pro-life, respecting the unborn child as a sentient being.

It is important to note that both of these women were psychologists who also had years of experience with meditation. We should not expect that a young teenager who is pregnant would, in a culture that sorely neglects training in inner practices, be able to communicate so well with the child. Though some might be able to do it with only the support of knowing such communication is possible.

What these two women accomplished can, however, serve to broaden our perspective on abortion. It can be a goal towards which we as a culture can work. With this path as an additional possibility the intensity of the abortion conflict can be greatly lessened.

Even with the vast increase of scientific knowledge of incarnate existence, it is important that we remain humble and be open to new possibilities, and to the mystery.

TREES

When my father showed me in 1965 the tree grown from a horse-chestnut he had planted as a boy, it seemed inconceivable to me that a person could live long enough for such a large tree to grow from seed.

Then in the 1993 I understood. I saw the oak trees grown from acorns my brother and I had planted about 40 years earlier in our little flower gardens. The trees were huge. I remembered the time when my tree had grown to be the same height I was. I had felt we were equals. Now I was dwarfed by these huge oak trees.

How many people get to to know a tree in this way? Probably very few. Maybe we would treat the Earth differently if more people had an intimate relationship with a tree!

Our gardens in 1949

The oaks in 1993

My father and uncle with the ivy-covered tree they had planted over 50 years earlier

MUD PUDDLES

A relationship with the Earth is best started early. Mother bought hip boots for my brother and me and sent us out to play whatever the weather.

As I type this it is raining for the first time in almost two months. I just stood out in it, splashed barefoot in the puddles, and got soaked.

Wonderful!!!

My mother playing in a brook with her brother about 1912

With my brother, well equipped for puddle play, about 1947

With my mother on a walk in the woods in 1984

Visiting at Lost Lake, north of Spokane — October 18, 1987

Five AM, eastern sky lighting up as I sit cosy with tea by the fire. A star is in the sky just above the horizon. As it moves (that is, as the earth turns) the star is poised momentarily at the tip of a fir tree across the lake.

Memories of Christmas trees — sparkling lights and exquisite tree needle lace. Doorways out of time and space into eternity.

Now the sky is lighter. The clouds begin to be the yellow that precedes the pink of sunrise. The moment of magic passes. Day begins. Yet I go into the day nourished by that moment of eternity, eternity in form. These are lessons on being born, going into day without being afraid of losing the spark of divinity known in the night

As I sing a morning song, the star finally merges into the lighted sky of today.

FOOTPRINTS

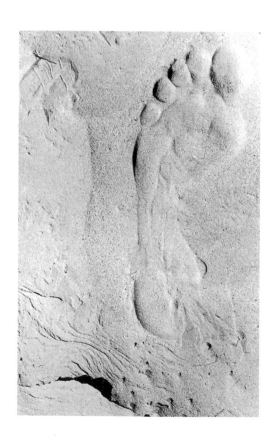

The writings and images in this book are like my footprints. Now, the thing about a foot print is that you can only see it when the person who made it is no longer standing in that place. So it is with what I have shared with you here. These are places I have been but no longer live in. Though I do still visit them occasionally. My journey continues, just not in this book!

I hope what you have seen here has both delighted you and helped to illuminate your own path through life.

Books written or edited by Jane English
Different Doorway: Adventures of a Caesarean Born
Childlessness Transformed

Books illustrated with photographs by Jane English
Tao Te Ching (with Gia-fu Feng)
Chuang Tsu: Inner Chapters (with Gia-fu-Feng)
Waterchild (with Judith Bolinger)
Mount Shasta: Where Heaven and Earth Meet (with Jenny Coyle)

Calendars with photographs by Jane English
Tao Calendar 2000
Mount Shasta 2000 Calendar
Ballooning 2000 Calendar
plus previous and future editions of these calendars

See the Earth Heart web page for more information on these titles
http://www.eheart.com

Secure online ordering through our friends at Village Books in Mt Shasta, CA
See http://www.eheart.com for a link to the Village Books order page.
Phone orders also through Village Books at 1-800-344-0436
Bookstores Nationwide
Most bookstores stock our publications, or can order them from the distributors listed below.
Distributors
APG 1-800-327-5113, also Ingram, Baker and Taylor, New Leaf, and Bookpeople